J. T. Trowbridge

The Scarlet Tanager and other Bipeds

J. T. Trowbridge

The Scarlet Tanager and other Bipeds

ISBN/EAN: 9783337062439

Printed in Europe, USA, Canada, Australia, Japan

Cover: Foto ©ninafisch / pixelio.de

More available books at **www.hansebooks.com**

THE SCARLET TANAGER

AND

OTHER BIPEDS

BY

J. T. TROWBRIDGE

BOSTON MDCCCXCII
LEE AND SHEPARD PUBLISHERS
10 MILK STREET NEXT "THE OLD SOUTH MEETING-HOUSE"
NEW YORK CHARLES T. DILLINGHAM
718 AND 720 BROADWAY

COPYRIGHT, 1891, J. T. TROWBRIDGE.

All Rights Reserved.

THE SCARLET TANAGER.

CONTENTS

	PAGE
THE SCARLET TANAGER	9
GRANDMOTHER'S GOLD BEADS	111
HILE HARDACK'S NEWFOUNDLAND PUP	147
PAUL GARWIN'S CHRISTMAS EVE	167

THE SCARLET TANAGER

CHAPTER I

THE PLEASURES OF EAVESDROPPING

On the grassy bank by the door of the old parsonage a slender boy, with thin, dark features and straight, black hair, sat with a shingle on his lap, skinning a bird.

Hearing the latch of the gate click, he looked up and scowled.

"It's old Pickerel!" he muttered, bending his eyes again intently on his work. "Wonder what he wants here!"

The visitor was a young man, not more than thirty; but, being a schoolmaster, the boys called him old; and, because his name was Pike, they called him Pickerel.

He came along the gravelled walk, swinging

his light cane, and without appearing to notice particularly the boy's occupation, said, in a tone of voice meant to be conciliatory, —

"Is your father at home, Gaspar?"

"No, he ain't," Gaspar replied curtly, without looking up again from his bird.

Old Pickerel — or, rather, young Mr. Pike — paused and hesitated, while a look of displeasure or disappointment, or both, gathered on that beaming, friendly face of his.

What he thought was: "When you come to my school, you'll be taught manners more becoming a minister's son, and learn not to say *ain't*." What he said was (in a tone still resolutely conciliatory, for he seemed aware of wild traits in this young colt, whom he was to catch first and afterward tame), —

"I am sorry for that. At what time will he return?"

"Don't know," said Gaspar shortly, as before, while he continued skinning his bird.

The visitor was about to turn away in disgust, but he hesitated again. It was evidently hard for him to keep up the bland and winning manner of his first questions; but he did it heroically, and asked if Gaspar's mother was in.

"Guess so," was the discourteous answer he received; and he moved on toward the door.

"If the old gentleman ain't at home, the old lady will do," mused Gaspar, who commonly spoke of his parents in this light, irreverent way. (Sometimes, I regret to relate, they were "the old man" and "the old woman.")

"What's up, I wonder? I'll bet they've sent for him to talk over my going into the high school this fall!"

He stopped skinning his bird, and fixed on vacancy a fierce, discontented look.

"But I ain't going to the high school; that's all there is about that! My days of slavery are over. I'm going to have a good time now, when I can; and when I can't, I'll make a row."

He tried to give his mind once more to the bird-skinning, but he was excited and listless; a longing possessed him to know how a quiet little conversation about himself would sound.

He seemed to conclude that it would be amusing; so, slipping the shingle, with the bird and knife on it, under a lilac-bush, he glided cautiously around the corner of the house, and turned up an expectant ear under the sitting-room window.

He could hear voices within, but it was some time before he could make out much that was said. At length his mother's voice began to rise and swell with tempestuous emotion.

"I wish my husband were here to talk with you," she was saying, "for I can't, — I can't, — without giving way to my feelings and saying what I know I shall regret afterward."

"You need not hesitate to be quite frank with me," was the reply, in earnest accents, breaking through the subdued tones of the formal call. "I know something about boys. I have studied them all my life, and I have never yet found one that did not have some good traits that could be successfully appealed to, if approached by the right person in the right way."

"It *is* about me," thought Gaspar, listening breathlessly. But he was not displeased by the visitor's remark. "Guess old Pick ain't such a very scaly fellow, after all!" he said to himself. But his mother was speaking now.

"Oh, yes! And Gaspar is no exception. He can be the pleasantest, most obliging boy you ever saw, when things go to suit him; but that isn't much of the time, I'm forced to say, if I *am* his mother! And when things don't go just according to his notion — oh! I can't begin to tell you how we suffer from his unfilial conduct!"

The mother's voice became flawed and gusty with grief; while the listener under the window scowled and set his teeth, as if he found eavesdropping not so agreeable a pastime as he had anticipated.

The schoolmaster made some sympathetic response, which was only half-audible to Gaspar, and then Mrs. Heth went on: —

"He seems to regard us as his enemies: whereas, mercy knows, we work and pray only for his good. He is not a malicious or a vicious boy; nor lazy, if he is only interested in what he is doing — then, I am often surprised to see how industrious and capable he is!"

"That is boy-like. I have known many just such cases," said the visitor.

"I shouldn't mind, if we could ever get him interested in anything we wish him to do," the mother resumed. "But that seems well-nigh impossible. The very fact that we wish a thing done is enough to prejudice him against it, and often we have induced him to pursue a desired course by appearing to oppose him in it. He told his sister that he couldn't be hired to go to the picnic last week; but when his father said, 'I suppose you won't care to go, and it will be better, perhaps, for you to stay at home,' he changed his mind and went, to our great relief."

"Ho, ho!" whispered Gaspar softly, not at all pleased to learn how he had been cajoled. "I'll look out for you next time!"

"His father and I have wished to give him an education; and though we are not rich, we would cheerfully have made any sacrifices to send him to college and prepare him for a profession. But he hates study. Oh! when I think of the difference between him and some boys I know, who are striving for an education against the greatest obstacles, while he is throwing away his opportunities, it makes me " —

"What is she crying for?" Gaspar said to himself, in the painful interval of silence which followed.

"We should be willing for him to leave school," she resumed presently, "if there were any other useful thing he would apply himself to. But he thinks he's cruelly misused if we even require him to take care of the horse, or split a little kindling-wood. It is, in fact, so great a trial to get anything of that kind done, that his father would never ask it of him if it were not a still greater trial to see him idle. That he is a minister's son makes the matter seem worse than if he belonged to anybody else: so much is expected of a minister's family! But he appears to have no regard for his father's position, and, indeed, but very little respect for him, anyway."

"I infer that he is not a very good scholar," said the visitor.

"He is a very poor scholar. But it isn't the

fault of his ability. I never saw a child so quick to learn, when he once gives his mind to anything. But his object in school seems to have been to have all the fun he could, while studying just enough to pass his examinations, and not get left by his class. Not one of his teachers has seemed able to get at the right side of him; and I know he has worked against them in every way he could."

"Evidently they have not understood him," said the schoolmaster.

"How could they be expected to understand him, when I, his own mother, cannot?" said the woman despondently. "Oh, what would I not give to find the right chord to touch in his nature, and know just how to reach it! There must be such a chord, — he is so bright, so ingenious, so ready to help almost anybody but his own family and friends!"

Gaspar scowled harder than ever, and his breath came thickly. He wished his mother would not talk in that way.

"You see, now," she went on, "why we have sent for you. We need your advice and help.

We are very anxious that he should enter at your school the next term; and I thought that perhaps, if you could talk with him, knowing something of his peculiar disposition to begin with, you might have some influence over him."

The schoolmaster did not reply for a moment.

"Guess he don't care to take that contract," thought Gaspar, remembering his recent surly behavior to the visitor. "He'll think that I'm too bad to try to do anything with, and I can't blame him." So he hardened his heart, although, for some reason, he felt now that he would a little rather have the good opinion of old Pickerel.

"What sort of persons are his associates?" the teacher asked after a pause.

"Just such as you might suppose,— the most idle and reckless boys in the neighborhood. There is Pete Cheevy, perhaps the worst of them all. Scarce a day passes but he and our boy are off together robbing birds' nests, or killing the poor little birds."

"I have observed them together," said the

visitor; "and I must confess that I have wondered to see your son keeping such company."

"We have tried to prevent it," rejoined the mother; "and we have tried to prevent this warfare on the birds. But Gaspar has a gun — an old-fashioned fowling-piece that his uncle gave him; he even feels hard toward us, because his father will not buy him a breech-loader! He says that we oppose him in everything. Whereas, mercy knows, we have been too indulgent. He is an only son; he was our idol in his babyhood, — all our hopes centred in him. Now, to think how he repays us!"

And Gaspar, under the window, could distinctly hear his mother's sobs.

"I am sure there must be some way of reaching his better nature," said Mr. Pike. "But I see he is suspicious of me, thinking, no doubt, that because I am a schoolmaster I must be plotting against his liberty. I will help you, if I can, Mrs. Heth; but it is possible that it will not be best for him to enter the high school; and, if so, for his own good we should wish to know it."

"He's a level-headed old Pick, anyway!" thought Gaspar, under the window.

"It isn't always wise to oppose such a boy in everything," the visitor went on. "But if we can discover the bent of his genius, and what he wishes most at heart, we may, perhaps, direct him in the right way, — not by damming the stream, but by turning it into a proper channel."

His voice sounded as if he was rising to go, and the boy made haste to get away from the window.

CHAPTER II

A TALK ABOUT BIRDS

When Mr. Pike came out of the house, a few minutes later, he saw Gaspar Heth sitting on the grass where he had left him, with the little raw, red body of the bird on the shingle beside him, and the skin in his hands, smoothing out the ruffled plumage.

"What sort of bird is that?" the schoolmaster inquired, approaching, and leaning on his cane.

Gaspar did not answer for a moment, undecided whether to regard this man as a friend or an enemy. He shaped the wings, and holdout the beak and tail, said at length, —

"Don't you know it?"

"No, I don't; I know very little about birds, — much less than I wish I did."

"It's a flicker," said Gaspar, quite pleased to

be able to teach the master of the high school something.

"A flicker? What's a flicker?" queried the master.

"A high-hole," said Gaspar.

"Well!" Mr. Pike answered good-humoredly, "that leaves me as ignorant as I was before. What is a high-hole?"

Gaspar laughed. It was fun to puzzle old Pickerel, and he wished some boys that he knew were there to witness his triumph.

"It's a yellow-hammer," he replied. "Now you know."

"Now I don't know; in fact, I know less than I did before," said the master. "For, if I am not mistaken, the yellow-hammer is a European species; we have no yellow-hammer in this country."

This bit of bird-knowledge took the gleeful Gaspar by surprise. He did not respect old Pick any the less for it, however.

"You are not mistaken," he said. "We have no true yellow-hammer. But that is one of the common names this bird goes by. It is called a flicker, too, I suppose, on account of the flashing yellow of its wings when it flies; and a high-hole, from the holes it makes for its nest in the trunks of trees."

"Now I know the bird," replied the schoolmaster; "as I think I should have done at first, if I had seen it on the wing. It is the pigeon-woodpecker, or golden-winged woodpecker, or golden-shafted woodpecker; it seems to have a great many names."

Gaspar was growing interested in the conversation.

"It has still another name," he said; "*you* ought to know that."

"Why so?"

"Because it is Latin, and because you are the schoolmaster."

"I am humiliated now!" said the teacher, with a humorous, rueful smile. "I pretend to teach Latin, and yet I don't know the Latin name for this bird!—though, I suppose, it must be some sort of *picus*, that being the Latin name for woodpecker."

"That's it," cried Gaspar, growing more and

more animated. "Though I have always called it *pick-us*, because it picks the trees."

"A very natural mistake," said the schoolmaster. "But the *i* has the long sound; and the word is not related to our word *pick* at all. This *picus* must have some other Latin word to qualify it, and show what particular species it is. Do you remember it?"

"*Auretus; pickus auretus*, or something like that."

The master smiled again.

"Not *au'retus*, but *aura'tus*, my boy, with the accent on the long *a* of the second syllable; *picus aura'tus*. That is, *woodpecker decked with gold;* and a very good name it is. I am not surprised that you did not get it quite right; on the contrary, I am surprised that you should have observed and remembered the Latin name at all."

"There's a book about birds in the public library; in looking it over, I've noticed that all the woodpeckers are called *picus*, — which I thought meant *pickers*, — and then I couldn't help wondering what some of the other words meant. I have asked myself what *auratus* stood for, a good many times; and now I am glad that I know it means 'decked with gold.' But I can't see the use of giving Latin and Greek names to birds and things, nowadays."

"Perhaps I can explain it to you," said the master. "Take this bird, for instance. We have seen that it has several common names; one of which, certainly, belongs to another bird. So, if a person speaks of a yellow-hammer, how are you to know whether he means this or the European species? In ordinary conversation you may think that is not very important; but in all scientific descriptions, it is necessary that such names shall be used as cannot be misunderstood."

"But why can't men of science agree upon English names?" the boy inquired.

"That is a sensible question. The answer to it is that all men of science are not English-speaking people. There are German, French, Spanish, Swedish, Dutch, Russian ornithologists, and those of many other countries. Now, it is true, they might all agree upon an English name for each bird; but it would be as unreasonable for us to expect that of foreigners, as we would consider it, if we were all required to learn a French or a Dutch name. It really seems much simpler and more convenient to use Latin and Greek names, which learned men in all countries agree upon and understand; so that a German man of science will know just what a Spanish man of science is writing about, if he uses correct scientific terms. Now, take the case of this very bird. A Swedish naturalist, named Linnæus, who was a great botanist, and classified and gave scientific names to plants, also gave names to many birds — to this species, I suppose, among others; so that, when *picus auratus* is alluded to by any writer in any language, ornithologists know just what bird is meant. So, you see, these scientific terms that you dislike form a sort of universal language understood by men of science the world over."

"Can't a person be a good ornithologist without knowing Latin and Greek?" Gaspar inquired.

"Oh, yes; but he will find it very useful indeed to know those languages, especially as some species of birds have more than one scientific name, given them by more than one writer on the subject. To know at least the rudiments of Greek and Latin will be a great help to him; and these can be acquired without very severe study. But, after all," the master continued, seeing the boy's countenance fall, "to know a thing itself is of much greater importance than to know fifty different names for it, be they ever so scientific. I suppose you have learned a great deal about this bird, its characteristics of form and color, its habits, its food, and its eggs."

"I know all that," said Gaspar, brightening again. "I have its eggs, and they are beauties! Six of them, pure white, about an inch long. I got them myself, by hard digging with a knife, out of a hole in a tree as long as my arm — I mean the hole, not the tree."

"But didn't you feel a little sorry to take away the eggs from the mother bird?" Mr.

Pike ventured to say, watching the boy's face carefully.

"I should have felt worse if I hadn't known she would keep right on and lay more, and hatch her brood just the same, only somewhat later. I wanted the eggs for my collection."

"Have you a collection? I should like to see it."

"Would you?" said Gaspar. "Well, I'd like to show it to you, if you won't mind the looks of my room. I am scolded every day in the year for the litter I keep it in, but I don't see what harm it does. I'll show you my collection of bird-skins, too, if you like." And, as the master replied that he would like that, too, very much, Gaspar led the way into the house.

CHAPTER III

GASPAR'S COLLECTIONS

Mrs. Heth had watched with anxious interest the schoolmaster and her wayward son talking together in the yard; but it was not without a feeling of dismay that she saw Gaspar bring in the visitor and start with him toward the chamber stairs.

"Gaspar!" she cried, "what are you going to do?"

"Show my collections," said Gaspar stiffly.

"He won't care for your collections, and, you know, you keep your room in such a state that I am positively ashamed to have it seen," remonstrated the mother.

"Excuse me, I have been in boys' rooms before," replied the master, "and I have a real desire to see his collections."

With a face full of apprehension and distress,

the good woman drew back into the sitting-room, thankful that she had at least prepared him for the untidy appearance of things, which the most careful and conscientious housekeeping could not permanently remedy.

Owing, perhaps, to that forewarning, Mr. Pike, on entering the chamber, did not appear to notice at all the oil-spots on the wall-paper, the scattered feathers and bits of cotton-wool and sticks and leaves on the carpet, clothing and shoes flung about, some loose matches on the bed, and a hammer and a handful of nails on a chair. He did not mean to be surprised at anything; and he was, perhaps, all the more surprised for that reason.

Gaspar began to open his bureau drawers, the contents of which accounted for a tumbled heap of shirts and socks, thrust into a box that peeped out from under the bed, all his wearing apparel having been removed to make space for the things, which, in his eyes, were of vastly greater importance. These were his collections; and it was the order and beauty displayed in their arrangement, contrasted with the great disorder of the room, which surprised the master.

There were eggs of various sizes, from those of the osprey and the great horned-owl down to those of the humming-bird and the smallest wren. The larger eggs were laid side by side in open pasteboard boxes. "For, of course, I couldn't bring home a night-heron's nest, or a fish-hawk's nest," Gaspar explained. "Guess such rafts of sticks and limbs would be too much, even for *my* room!" Some of the smaller eggs, also, were in boxes. "For it happens, sometimes, that two or three of us will discover a rare nest, and, of course, only one can have it; but we can share the eggs, if it has more than one."

Most of the eggs, however, were in their native nests, which were arranged with neatness and taste. These were of a great variety of size and structure, from that of the ruby-throated humming-bird, so diminutive and dainty, — (a soft bunch of the gathered down of plants, having delicately colored lichens stuck all over it, except in the thimble-like hollow which contained the two pearls of lovely white eggs) — from that small miracle of bird-architecture, resembling a knot on a limb, to the larger and coarser nests woven of strings and sticks and hair.

Mr. Pike noted these differences with a great deal of interest, and finally exclaimed, —

"What's this? It looks like a sort of two-story nest, with eggs above and below."

"That's just what it is," replied Gaspar, delighted to see the interest with which the master regarded his treasures. "Do you see through it?"

"I see through it, in one sense," Mr. Pike replied; "for the upper story seems to have been rather hastily constructed. But it's a puzzle to me. There's one egg in the lower nest, lighter colored and much larger than the other two."

"The nest is the chipping-sparrow's," said Gaspar; "sometimes called the hair-bird's, because it is nearly always lined with horse-hair. The two small, bluish-green eggs in the lower story are the bird's own; the larger one is that of a stranger, the meanest of all birds, — the cow-bunting, which lays its eggs in the nests of other birds."

"I thought that was the habit of the cuckoo," observed the master.

"It may be of the European cuckoo," said Gaspar; "I have heard that it is. But our American cuckoos build nests of their own. Here is one, built of twigs and leaves and moss, — the black-billed cuckoo's, — which I found myself."

The master examined the nest, but did not appear quite convinced.

"Are you sure?" he asked. "Emerson says, —

> "'Yonder masterful cuckoo
> Crowds every egg out of the nest,
> Quick or dead, except its own.'

"And by 'yonder cuckoo,' an American writer could hardly have meant a bird across the ocean, if he knew what he was talking about, as Emerson generally did."

"But he didn't, if he was talking about our native cuckoos," Gaspar declared confidently.

The schoolmaster smiled to see this black-eyed boy brush aside the words of the Concord philosopher with a disdainful gesture. Gaspar went on: —

"I've watched the birds ever so many times; and don't I know? The cow-bunting is the rogue! I saw the bird go to this sparrow's nest, when there were two sparrow eggs in it, and it left that third egg. But it didn't crowd out the others; it left its own to be hatched with them, and the young bird to be taken care of by the sparrow, along with her own young, until it had outgrown them, and shouldered them out of their own nest, as it would have been sure to do after a while. But what did the sparrow do? She saw that it was a strange egg, but didn't know how to get rid of it; so she set to work with her mate to build the upper story of the nest, and got it ready in time to lay her next egg in it. But they had done their work in too great a hurry; it was open to criticism, as you see. So they abandoned it, and I took it for my collection."

"It is very curious!" said the master.

Three drawers contained the nests and eggs. Gaspar opened a fourth, in which were displayed the smallest of his bird-skins. Each had the beak and claws attached, and was wrapped about a slender, artificial body of cotton-wool, and laid on its back. The different specimens of a species — the male and female and young — were ranged side by side; those of the species nearest akin were placed next; and so on, through each family, sub-family, and order. It was a wonderful sight; all were so beautiful, all so still; not like dead birds, but rather like birds in a trance or sleep. The larger birds were ranged in like manner in broad pasteboard boxes.

"Do you know all these species and their eggs?" the master inquired.

"Oh, of course!" said Gaspar carelessly. "It took me a long while to learn all the warblers and their eggs; for there are a great many of them, and some are very much alike. These are the warblers," he added, spreading his hands over a row of the smaller birds, "the chestnut-sided, the blue yellow-backed, the blue-winged yellow, the black-poll, the black-throated blue, the Cape May, the yellow-rumped, the " —

"Never mind about the rest!" exclaimed the master. "I am surprised that you should have studied and collected so many specimens."

"The only way to study them is to collect them," replied Gaspar. "Now, some folks are interested in books. But what I am interested in is birds."

"You should be a naturalist," observed the master.

"Oh! that's what I should like to be!" said the boy, his dark features glowing with enthusiasm. "But, no, — my folks want to make something else of me. They think the time I spend studying birds is 'time thrown away.' I am 'idling;' and I am a 'cruel wretch' because I take eggs and nests."

"But do you not think, yourself, that it is a great pity to destroy so many eggs and birds?" asked the master. "You have a beautiful display here; but do you know what struck me at first? Not the beauty, but the pity of it! I am glad I have seen it, for now I know there is another side to the question than that of wanton destruction and cruelty."

"Wanton destruction and cruelty!" cried Gaspar, his eyes flashing. "I never take a bird nor an egg that I don't need to complete my collection. I only get my share, and hardly that. If you could see the host of real enemies one of these little sparrows has to dodge and hide away from before she can make a nest and raise her brood! minks and snakes, and red squirrels, and weasels, and hawks, and jays, and butcher-birds, and owls, and cats, and "—

"And young collectors," put in the master, in a quiet tone.

"I own," said Gaspar, "that they are about the worst enemies that birds have, after all! I don't mean the real collectors, for I believe they are the birds' best friends."

"I think the true ornithologist is a friend to the birds, as he must be their lover," the master admitted. "But you know, Gaspar, as well as I do, that 'collecting' is a mania with boys; innocent enough when confined to autographs and postage-stamps, but harmful when it leads to the destruction of living creatures, with no noble end in view. How many boys do you know who have begun collections of birds and eggs that will never have the least scientific value, but will be neglected and flung out-of doors in a year or two?"

"How many? lots of them!" Gaspar answered frankly. "But I am not one of 'em."

"You go with them, however?"

"Yes, I go with them sometimes, for their company and help. There's that Pete Cheevy; he can climb trees like a squirrel, and I've some rare nests I could never have got without his assistance. By going with me, he has picked up a lot of eggs and nests; but it's just waste material for such a fellow; all that a collection is to him is just something to brag of.'

"Don't you think it is a great evil, Gaspar? Where is the law against such things?" inquired the schoolmaster.

"Boys in this town care nothing for the law; they're in no danger, as long as there's nobody to complain of them. But I wish myself, sometimes, that the law might be enforced, — provided my father would get me a permit to take birds and eggs for scientific purposes," the boy hastened to add.

"Are you sure that your purposes are scientific?" the master inquired.

Gaspar looked down thoughtfully at his row of fly-catchers, smoothed the breasts of the chebec and the wood pewee in an absent minded sort of way, then suddenly turned his dark eyes on the master.

"What do you think?" he asked.

Before answering, Mr. Pike put to him a few questions as to his methods of preserving the eggs and birds, or, rather, the shells and skins; and especially as to the marks by which he distinguished species and ascertained the names of birds new to him.

Gaspar described the process of blowing an egg, and of curing a skin; then proceeded to deliver so intelligent and entertaining a lecture upon beaks and shanks and wing-coverts, and mandibles, *tarsi* and primaries, that Mr. Pike listened with surprise and pleasure.

"Really, Gaspar," he said, "you show the zeal

and instinct of a naturalist. I don't wonder you find the pursuit fascinating. How many more of our native birds will it take to complete your collections?"

"I want particularly a scarlet tanager, and a yellow-billed cuckoo, and five or six more," replied the boy; "with about as many rare nests and eggs."

"Now, Gaspar," rejoined the master, "I have a proposition to make, in your own interest, as well as that of the birds. You must agree with me that the wholesale destruction of birds and eggs by boys who have no scientific knowledge of the subject, and do not aspire to have, ought to be prohibited."

"Yes, sir," Gaspar admitted.

"Now, I want you to unite with me in helping to put a stop to it."

"But — what — how can I?"

"We will get up an interest in the subject among the townspeople, especially among the boys; and, if necessary, we will call the attention of the proper authorities to it; for the destruction of the birds, you know, means the destruction of our forests and orchards and crops by injurious insects, which our feathered friends help to keep down. We will see, Gaspar, if we cannot get this useful and humane law enforced."

The boy's face looked gloomy.

"In return for what you do," the master continued, "I think I shall be able to get you a certificate from the officers of the Natural History Society, which will allow you to take birds and eggs for strictly scientific purposes."

The boy's face brightened.

"Now, that is fair, is it not?" said Mr. Pike, in a cheery tone.

"Yes — but — I don't know!" stammered Gaspar. "It will be hard for me to go back on the fellows who have hunted birds and nests with me before now."

"You needn't 'go back on them,' as you say, or do anything mean and dishonorable. But what is to prevent your telling them that a movement is on foot to enforce the law, and that you, for one, intend to obey the law in future?"

Gaspar laughed with those bright black eyes of his.

"They wouldn't believe me!"

"What, have you so bad a reputation as a law-breaker? I am sorry to hear it! But you can mend it by mending your practices, and soon teach the boys that you are in earnest. Now promise me that you will help on by word and example the movement I propose, and I promise to get you the permit."

After some hesitation, Gaspar made the promise. Mr. Pike gave him his hand.

"I am very glad that I have had this talk with you, Gaspar. And now I am going to tell you frankly that I really came here to-day to consult with your parents about your entering the high school."

"I knew you did," said Gaspar, rather shamefacedly.

"And that is the reason why you were, perhaps, a little short with me as I came in? Well, never mind; you would have been more courteous, perhaps, if you had understood me better. I am not going to urge your parents to send you to school, unless you see yourself that you ought to go. Whatever you make of yourself in life, you will find a little more education than you now have extremely useful; and especially if you mean to be an ornithologist, you should acquire a good, liberal, general knowledge, and learn how to describe your observations and discoveries with correctness and force. Think of it, will you? Meanwhile, I will talk with your parents, and help them to a better understanding of you and your aims than they now have. Remember your promise, Gaspar, about the boys and birds!"

Mr. Pike afterward talked again with Mrs. Heth, and gave her much comfort and encouragement regarding her son. He lost no time in applying for the certificate, which he had promised, on his part; and, when he found that a small fee for it was required, gladly paid it out of his own pocket. In the mean time, he became better acquainted with Gaspar, and had good reason to believe that his influence might do much toward reforming the boy, and likewise in preserving the birds of the neighborhood from wanton destruction.

Everything was, in fact, going on favorably when Gaspar one day suddenly disappeared, — disappeared as mysteriously and completely as if he had vanished in air, or had been swallowed up by the earth.

What strange thing had happened to him will be told in a future chapter.

CHAPTER IV

HOW GASPAR BROKE HIS PROMISE

I SAID everything was going on favorably. But it could not be expected that a boy like Gaspar would change the habits of his life and his whole mode of thought in a day or a week. He was impatient to see the promised certificate, the idea of which tickled his boyish pride; and as he did not know the reason why it was delayed, he more than once had resolved to break off his connection with the schoolmaster and go back to his wild associates.

His behavior to his parents was a little more considerate than it had been, but it was still perverse. The minister was a rather silent man, and he had so long regarded his son with gloomy dissatisfaction, that he could not easily take the first steps toward a better understanding. Yet his heart had softened toward him, and he, too, with the mother, hoped for good results from the teacher's influence.

A little more than a week had passed. It was Saturday afternoon, and Mr. Heth was absent from home, when Gaspar took his gun and started for the woods; there was a load in in it, which he wished to fire off. His sister Ella called after him.

"You are not going a-hunting, are you?" she asked.

"I am. What have you got to say about it?" he retorted haughtily.

She was a year and a half younger than he, but old enough to see how wrong his conduct often was, and to wish he would mend it.

"Now, Gaspar," she cried, "you know it isn't right! Papa said you must be sure to trim those borders, for to-morrow is Sunday."

"There'll be time enough for the borders when I get back," he scowlingly replied. "So don't fret, little schoolma'am."

"That's what you always say, 'time enough.' You put off your work to the last, and then it is never done. You'll not touch those borders to-day; I know you'll not," she cried, "if you don't do them now."

"You'll see! I can't be gone long, for I've no ammunition. I am not to be ordered around by you, anyhow!" And Gaspar stalked off.

"Don't say anything more to him," the mother called to Ella. "He will have his way."

"I suppose so," said Ella; "he always has had it, and he always will have it. But it provokes me!" And she stood in the doorway, gazing after him with sparkling dark eyes.

In the lane leading to the wood Gaspar caught glimpses of a ragged fellow lurking behind some bushes.

"Hallo, Pete!" he cried. "What are you hiding there? Where did you get that melon?" he added, as Pete Cheevy, recognizing him, came out from his ambush with a cantaloupe in his grimy hands.

"Found it rollin' up-hill, lookin' fer an owner," said the grinning Pete. "Set down here, an' we'll rip her open an' hev a jolly treat."

"Hello, Pete! Where did you get that Melon?"
Page 46.

It was a temptation. But Gaspar had been shunning the Cheevy urchin for a week, and he was not to be drawn back to him now by the bribe of a melon which he knew must have been stolen.

"No, thank you," he replied, walking on.

"Thought you tol' me las' Sat'day you wa'n't go'n' ter shoot any more birds, now't they talk o' tight'nin' up the law on 'em," observed Pete.

"I'm not," said Gaspar, thinking how Pete and the other fellows would envy him when he had his certificate. "But I may pick up a blue jay; there's no law about them."

"I'll go 'long with ye 'f ye want me ter," Pete proposed.

Gaspar reflected that the egg-hunting season was over, and he needed no assistance in climbing trees.

"Say, shell uh?" (Ragged urchin's phrase for "shall I?")

"Not with that melon," Gaspar replied significantly.

"Never mind the melon! I'll hide it till we come 'long back." But as Gaspar walked on without more words, Pete bawled after him: "Seems t'me somebody's awful stiff all t'once! Go 'long 'th yer ol' gun! I don' wan' ter shoot it. An' ye sha'n't hev any o' my mushmelon, nuther."

He pulled out from the pocket of his tattered trousers a knife with half a blade, and proceeded to "rip her open," as he phrased it, under a clump of bushes, where he regaled himself, devouring greedily all the good part of the melon and throwing away the rinds. Then he rose up, stretched himself, wiped his fingers on his trousers and his face on his sleeve, and, hardly knowing what else to do for amusement that afternoon, followed Gaspar up into the woods.

"Pleg' on the feller! dunno' what's got inter him!" he muttered. "He'll come roun' mebby, 'f I ask him 'f he don't want any kingfisher's eggs; he was pesterin' me fer 'em las' month."

The woods were very still that afternoon, and Gaspar went a long way without seeing or hearing any but the commonest birds. Not a

woodpecker drummed, not a jay screamed.
But at length, when he was about a mile from
home, in the most ancient part of the forest,
where still a few very old trees grew along
with those of a younger generation, his quick
ear detected a sound which made him stop
short and raise his gun.

It was something like a robin's song, and yet
he knew it was not a robin's. Two or three
times before he had heard it in deep woods,
and had caught glimpses of the brilliant plumage of the bird which uttered it. It came
now from the sun-spotted foliage high above his
head, into which he gazed eagerly, trembling
with excitement, sure that a prize which he
had long sought in vain was at last within his
reach.

The song was repeated, and then something
like a winged flame darted among the branches;
only the wings were not flame-like. Black
wings and tail, and a body as red as fire, — O
joy! It was the one bird he most desired of all,
so rare in all that region — *the Scarlet Tanager!*

I cannot say that Gaspar forgot his promise

to the master. But though his permit had not come, he believed it ought to have come; "and it's probably on the way now, if it's coming at all," he reasoned, while he watched eagerly for a good shot. "Anyhow, I'm not going to let a male Scarlet Tanager escape me, permit or no permit, law or no law!"

He saw a movement of the bright carmine breast through a screen of leaves, drew a quick aim, and fired.

The bird dropped from its perch, but seemed partially to recover the use of its wings before it had fallen far, and alighted, or rather lodged, in the fork of one of the largest old trees in the forest.

It was an oak, the main stem of which had, years before, been broken off about twenty feet from the ground. But from that point two living limbs still grew: one very large, branching toward the south, and a smaller one pushing out in the opposite direction, both rising high among the surrounding tree-tops.

It was in the hollow between these two limbs that the bird had fallen, and well out of sight, as Gaspar found by walking two or three times around the tree.

"A rare bird like that — it is too bad to lose it!" he said, gazingly wistfully up at the spot. "But of course nobody can shin up a trunk like that. What a fool I was not to let Pete come with me! I would make him help me bring a ladder; or he might get on that smaller limb from the branches of this little pine. Pete's such an exasperating fellow!" he exclaimed impatiently. "Why isn't he here when he's wanted?"

Having no second charge for his gun, he laid it on a mossy log, where he sat down to wait for the bird to show itself again, and to consider what he should do.

CHAPTER V

PETE CHEEVY AND THE GUN

At dusk that evening the minister, in his dressing-gown with his black study-cap on his head, — for he was bald,— was pacing to and fro before his door, when Mr. Pike came in at the gate.

Mr. Heth looked up quickly, with a perturbed and lowering face, as if expecting somebody else, and at sight of the schoolmaster made an effort to appear unconcerned and gracious.

After a few commonplace words of greeting had been passed between them, Mr. Pike, declining an invitation to enter the house, took an envelope from his pocket, saying, —

"I have called to see Gaspar; I have something which I think will please him."

"What is it?" the minister demanded sharply.

"The permit I promised him," replied the

caller, wondering what new shadow of trouble had come over the household, "the permit from the Natural History Society."

"He don't deserve it!" Mr. Heth broke forth with strong feeling. "He is the most undutiful, ungrateful boy I ever saw! I wonder at myself for expecting better things of him, after his behavior in the past."

Surprised and pained, the master could only ask, "Has anything new occurred, Mr. Heth?"

"Nothing new," replied the agitated father. "It's the same old story. But it is all the more exasperating just at this time, when we had hopes, — were beginning to have hopes, — after your talks with him, and his improved behavior, as if he really meant to do better; but I give him up! I give him up! I find I can place no reliance whatever upon him."

"I can't bear to think he has driven you to that conclusion," said the master in tones of sympathy and distress. "Where is he now?"

"That's what I don't know. I haven't seen him since I left home at about two o'clock. I gave him a light task to do, — a very light task,

— but told him to be sure to do it; for I wished to try him again and see if there was any conscience or obedience in the boy. He promised heartily; but at about three o'clock he took his gun and went off — no one knows where. His sister Ella reminded him of his work; but he answered her in his usual way, — that he would be back in time for it, that it was no affair of hers, and that she wasn't his guardian, or in words to that effect. He has not been home since."

"He must return now very soon," observed the schoolmaster. "It is too late to shoot anything."

"And it is too late to do his work," said the minister. "He may come now when he pleases. I could almost say, in my wrath and grief, that I care little whether he comes or not. But no, no! In spite of everything, I still have his good at heart. Come in. His mother will be glad to see you. By your interest in him, misplaced as it has been, you have won something more than her esteem."

"I cannot think my interest has been misplaced," Mr. Pike replied, rallying from his first discouragement. "I have great confidence that a boy of his fine ability and love of nature will come out all right. I think something has occurred to detain him. I will go in and wait a little while."

He remained an hour, — two hours. It was half-past nine o'clock, and Gaspar had not returned. It was not an unusual thing for the boy to be absent so late, although that had commonly happened, heretofore, when he had gone out after supper. He did not often get his supper away from home, and the evening meal was something that held an important place in his esteem. Mr. Pike could not wonder that Mrs. Heth was growing more and more anxious for her son's safety.

"Pete Cheevy, if anybody, will be apt to know where he is," she remarked as the visitor at last rose to go.

"I think so," said he; "and if there is a light in the house as I go up the street, I will call and make inquiries."

The Cheevys lived in a little old house under

the brow of a wooded hill that rose abruptly, with steep, half-hidden ledges, a few rods back from the street. There was no light visible as Mr. Pike approached the place, and he concluded that the family had gone to bed. But looking back, after he had passed, he saw a glow in an upper room under the low gable, the window of which was open.

He hesitated a minute, unwilling to disturb the family; but seeing a shadow pass the window, and thinking the chamber might be Pete's, he entered the yard and leaned against a bank-wall under the cliff. The moon was just rising; the rocks and overhanging woods were picturesquely touched with light; but everything was still, except for the sound of the master's own movements and the shrill notes of the tree-crickets.

Again the shadow crossed the casement, and, to make sure that it was Pete in the room, the master mounted the bank-wall. He was rewarded for the effort by seeing our young acquaintance, by the light of a not very brilliant lamp, performing some queer antics with a gun: now petting it as if it were some living creature, now taking aim at some imaginary game, and again trying the lock as if he found in its mechanism a wonderful fascination.

"One would think he had never seen a gun before," the master said to himself, standing high on the bank to get a better view. "Peter!" he called in a loud whisper.

Peter did not hear; he was pulling up the hammer for another imaginary shot. This time his game seemed to be out of the window, toward which he made a sudden dash, pointing the muzzle in the direction of the schoolmaster.

"Peter!" called the latter in a sharp, warning voice.

Pete stopped as if he himself had received a shot, and in an instant boy and gun had disappeared in the chamber. Mr. Pike waited in silence, and in a little while saw a head cautiously advance to the casement and peer out into the half-moonlit night.

"Peter!" The head drew quickly back. "Peter Cheevy!" Peter now came again to the window, but without the gun.

"Who be ye, 'n' wha' d'ye want?" he said in a startled voice.

"I am Mr. Pike, and I want to know if you have seen Gaspar Heth this afternoon?"

"Me? How sh'd I see him? D'd you say Gaspar Heth?"

"Yes, I did say Gaspar Heth," said the master. "Where did you see him last?"

"Dunno. Haven't seen him lately — not much — not very lately. Though I b'lieve I did," Pete continued, recovering from his embarrassment, and assuming a tone of the utmost candor, — "now I rec'lect, I did see him goin' up into the woods to-day."

"What time?"

"I dunno. Some time t'day. Guess this aft'noon. Yes, I'm sure t'was this aft'noon. Why?"

"Because he hasn't come home, and his folks are anxious about him."

"Be they? Sho! Guess Gap Heth can take care o' himself; he gener'ly 'most alluz could. He's nobody's fool, Gap Heth!" observed Pete philosophically.

"Did he have his gun with him?" the schoolmaster inquired.

"I disremember; somehow I can't rec'lect 'bout the gun. Though 't seems t' me he *did* hev his gun. Yes, I'm pretty sure on't, come t' think."

"And you went a little way with him?"

"Me? No, I jes' didn't! Ketch me! Gap Heth's snubbed me lately, 'n' I'm not go'n' to tag aft' him!"

"What has he snubbed you for?"

"What fer? I don't know, 'n' I don't care! Talks 'bout you 'n' some folks screwin' up the law on bird-huntin'. That don't trouble me. Bird's-eggin' time's over, 'n' I don't shoot."

"Don't shoot?" cried the master. "I imagined you did, by the way I saw you handling your gun just now."

Pete made no reply to this simple remark; and if the light had been favorable for such a display, he might have been seen to roll his eyes and open his mouth with a ghastly attempt at a grin.

"So you haven't seen him since this afternoon, when he was going into the woods?" urged the master. "You are very sure?"

"Oh, yis! pos'tive sure!" Pete exclaimed, as if relieved to have the conversation come back to the main topic. "Tell ye 'f I hed; course I would! why shouldn't I?"

Although suspicious that the boy knew something about Gaspar that he was unwilling to tell, Mr. Pike did not press him further with questions; nor did he think it necessary to go back and inform the Heths of the ill-success of his attempt to get news of their son.

CHAPTER VI

MASTER PETE EXPLAINS

THE next morning, however, on his way to church, the master turned in at the parsonage gate. He felt sure the boy must be at home by that time; but the first anxious face that met him at the door told a different tale.

It was the face of the mother. "Have you heard from him?" she tremulously inquired.

"Not a word, except that the Cheevy boy saw him going into the woods yesterday afternoon."

As he followed her into the entry she said to him with quivering lips, "Do you believe it possible he has run away?"

No; he could not believe that.

"Or that he has met with some accident — with his gun?"

Mr. Pike thought that more probable, but refrained from saying so.

"I don't know what to think," he replied. "I will walk up into the woods and see if I can find any trace of him."

"His father has already been to look for him," said Mrs. Heth. "We had a terrible night; and at daylight he set off, exploring the woods and calling at neighbors' houses, where our poor boy might have been seen. But Mr. Heth came home all tired out. He is lying down now for a little rest. How he is going to get through his sermon this forenoon, I don't know."

Although these words were spoken in a fluttering voice, hardly above a whisper, they roused the minister in his room above, and he called from the door, —

"Is that Gaspar, or any news of him?"

"No; it is Mr. Pike; he is going into the woods to look for Gaspar," replied Mrs. Heth.

"It's no use," the minister replied. "I believe the boy has taken himself out of the way."

Nevertheless, Mr. Pike went to the woods, and spent the time he had intended for church in searching rocks and hollows for what he dreaded to find.

Mrs. Heth remained at home, vainly hoping to see her son come back. But the father, mastering his agitation, and nerving himself for the performance of duty, stood that morning as usual in the pulpit and bravely went through with prayer and sermon, — a pathetic figure to those who knew what grief and apprehension were at his heart.

In the meanwhile the schoolmaster, having spent an hour in unavailing search, bethought him to find Pete Cheevy again, in order to get that experienced youth to show him some of Gaspar's favorite haunts.

Pete was not at home; but his father was, — a sort of enlarged edition of Pete himself, slouching, tattered, unkempt, — who stared innocently enough when told of Gaspar's disappearance.

"I hadn't heard a word on't!" he said.

"I supposed everybody in town had heard of it by this time. And I should think Pete would have told you," remarked the schoolmaster.

"Guess Pete don't know it," replied the elder Cheevy, standing in his doorway, and fumbling his unbuttoned vest.

"Oh, yes, he does; for I stopped last night and told him Gaspar hadn't been heard from at half-past nine o'clock."

"Half-pas' nine? What're talkin' 'bout? My boy was abed and asleep 'fore that time."

"I beg your pardon," said the master; "I saw him through the window, in his room, playing with his gun."

"Ye're gett'n' things mixed up now, fer cert'n!" said the paternal Cheevy. "My boy hasn't any gun."

A sudden suspicion flashed across the master's mind. He was silent for a moment; then he said, —

"I can't be mistaken about the gun; and I think you will find it in his room now, if you will go and look. I certainly saw it last night.

"Can't be!" said the elder Cheevy. "But I'll go 'n' look, an' if I find he's keep'n' a gun without lett'n' me know on't, that boy'll ketch ginger, an' no mistake!"

He went tramping up the carpetless stairs in his thick-soled shoes, and was afterward heard asking his wife if she had seen Pete "hev any gun aroun' the house?" Mr. Pike awaited his return with great anxiety, believing that at last he had a clew to the mystery.

Mr. Cheevy came out, looking puzzled.

"Mus' be some mistake," he said. "Pete hasn't got a gun, and we can't find any gun."

Mr. Pike withdrew; and when, a little later, the younger Pete came slipping down the ledges, out of the woods, he was rushed upon, captured, and held fast with one hand by the elder Pete, who brandished an apple-tree branch with the other.

"How 'bout that gun?" demanded the irate Mr. Cheevy.

"O Pa! don't thrash me, an' I'll tell ye all 'bout it, — I will, sure!" screeched the junior, beginning to dance before the instrument began to play. "O Pa! O Pa!"

"Stop yer yellin'! I hevn't touched ye," said old Pete.

"But ye're goin' ter!" cried young Pete. "It's Gap Heth's gun, an' I found it on a log in the woods yest'day, an' I jes' brought it hum to keep it fer him, 's sure as I live and breathe this minute!"

"Be them the fac's?" said the father. "Don't you dare try to give me anything else but the genooine fac's! No triflin' with *me*, you know."

As the instrument seemed about to strike up a vivacious air, Pete danced again, swinging around the circle of which the radius was the paternal arm. At last, when he seemed to be sufficiently terrified to tell the truth, he was ordered to "stan' still an' tell it." This was his statement: —

"I saw Gap a-goin' up int' the woods with his gun, an' by 'n' by I follered him; but I couldn't get a sight on him, no way; I never seen him once, an' I dunno where he went. But over by Bingham's Swamp I come across his gun a-layin' on a log; an' he wasn't anywheres aroun', an' there wasn't anybody in sight, an' I'd never had a gun, an' that seemed my only chance, an' I took it."

"Hooked it, you mis'ble man's boy!" exclaimed old Pete.

"I didn't mean it fer hookin'; I *found* it!" young Pete exclaimed.

"Wall, that's another thing," said the father, softening. "Anybody's li'ble to *find* things. But why didn't you tell *me?*"

"I didn't know's ye'd lemme keep it," whimpered the boy.

"Now see what a scrape you're gettin' inter by not tellin'!" said his father. "When Schoolmaster Pike talked about yer gun this mornin', I told him, o' course, that you hadn't any gun. Where is 't now?"

"I got scared, an' hid it under some bushes up int' the woods, fus' thing this mornin'. Old Pickerel scared me las' night."

"Wall, you git it, an' kerry 't back to where ye found-it, lively! I don't want any boy o' mine hauled up fer findin' things that there's go'n to be so much fuss about as there is 'bout this, now Gap has got lost. Don't you see, if anything's happened ter him, ye might be put in jail fer murder? S'pose he's found shot, an' his gun found in your hands! Now you scamper an' git rid on't in a hurry; an' mind, ye leave it jes' where ye found it. Now scud!"

CHAPTER VII

THE HOLLOW TREE

Owing to the terrors of the situation, Pete had told a tolerably straightforward story. He had found the gun on a log, in the way he described. It was the same mossy log upon which Gaspar had sat down to wait for the scarlet tanager to show itself again, and to consider what he should do.

As the bird did not show itself, and as he knew nothing of Pete's following him into the woods, he finally said to himself, "I guess what Pete can do, I can do. I know he could shin up this pine and get off on the oak, and I believe I can."

It was a slender pine, about eight inches through, with a tendency to die at the top, which top, by the way, had had the misfortune to be thrust up into the branches of larger and taller trees. One of these was the great oak with the broken stem, at the summit of which, in the fork of the trunk, the scarlet tanager had lodged.

Gaspar himself was a good climber, as well as a resolute boy. He laid his gun across the log, hugged the pine with knees and arms, and began to work his way upward. He reached the branches without difficulty, and scrambled through them into the scraggly top, above which the smaller limb of the oak made a tremendous sweep, nearly twenty feet from the broken trunk.

In passing the dead or dying twigs of the pine-tops, he lost his cap, which lodged in them. "Never mind," he said, "I can get that on my way back." He looked over at the fork of the huge oak, but could not see his bird, — only the decayed hollow into which it had fallen. To reach it, by clasping the limb curved above him, and descending over that, in mid-air, was a feat which made him hesitate. Then he said, "Here goes!" and balancing himself in the pine-top, he stretched up his arms until he could clasp them securely over the oaken limb.

After his arms, up went his legs: and holding fast to the branch with hands and feet, he began to work his way down to the trunk, pausing to look back at the pine, and assure himself that his return that way would be safe.

"Yes," he said, "I can get back as easily as I came." And he slipped daringly down the great limb to the fork.

On reaching it he found that the broken stem contained, inside the ring of living wood and bark, a rotten cavity, into which the bird must have disappeared. The hole was large at the top, but it narrowed below; and there, looking down, he saw his bird clinging with half-spread wings to the decayed lining of the trunk.

"What a beauty!" he exclaimed; "I must have him sure!"

He rested with one arm about the limb he had descended, and cautiously thrust the other down into the hollow. With his utmost straining he could not reach the prize with his hand.

"Perhaps," thought he, "I can reach him with my foot."

So he got one leg into the cavity, and put it carefully down, his object being to place his foot beneath the bird, which seemed stupefied or exhausted, and force it gently upward.

"If he flies out," reasoned the boy, "he will fall to the ground, and I can catch him."

But instead of flying out, the tanager, roused by the pressure of the foot, fluttered still farther down, and clung again to a projection of the decayed lining.

"I shall lose him that way," Gaspar exclaimed. "I shall lose him anyway, unless I can reach him with my hand. I wish I had a string or something to make a slip-noose!"

The sight of the rich red body and velvety black tail and wings inspired him with that enthusiastic eagerness to possess the specimen which only a naturalist can understand.

Then he ventured on a rash undertaking, believing that he could let himself down into the hollow beside the bird until it would be easy to grasp it. This he did, forcing his toes into the rotten wood, — if anything so far gone in decay can be called wood, — and keeping as firm a hold as he could of the top of the opening.

When he thought he had gone far enough, he held on by his feet and one upstretched hand, and reached down with the other. There was the bird still; but he had hardly touched it, when it fluttered off again, and he made a sudden, fatal movement to grasp its wing.

The hold of hand and feet on the decayed wood gave way, and he slipped down into the narrow part of the cavity.

There, by desperately spreading legs and arms, and clutching his fingers into the soft lining, he managed for a while to support himself.

He looked up; his head was about three feet from the top of the opening. It was impossible to seize the rotten rim again. The space below was large enough to let his body slide down, but too small to allow him to use his legs and feet to any advantage. And the punklike substance into which he thrust his fingers was too slight to yield him much support.

He had been terrified by his first slip. And now he began to realize the horror of his situation.

He could wedge his knees and elbows into the cavity so that the slipping was arrested. But it began again the moment he tried to work his way upward.

There seemed to be nothing he could do but to hold himself in place and scream for help. And scream he did, with what strength he had left. But he soon perceived the futility of any such efforts. His voice was projected upward into the forest-tops and pitiless blue sky; it could not have been heard far in any other direction.

It was a terrible moment to a boy so full of life and hope but a little while before, but whom a sudden and awful death now threatened.

His strength began to fail; he could not even scream any more; he could only think. And all the while he was slowly slipping, slipping.

He thought of his home, which he had often

threatened to leave in hate and scorn, but which appeared a paradise to him now. If he were only there again! It seemed far off and strange; while his collections of birds and eggs, lately so real and all-important to him, faded into a sickening dream.

Then he thought of his parents, whose kindness he had so often repaid with ingratitude, and he called out in his agony, —

"O father! help me! help! help!"

But his father was probably at that moment riding quietly along the village street, thinking perhaps of his perverse son, whom he had left at home to do a trifling task which that son had neglected, and now could never do.

He remembered the prayers his mother taught him in childhood to repeat, but which he had utterly neglected in his later, reckless years. He wished he could pray now, for perhaps the angels might help him. But it seemed to him as if he had never prayed; certainly his heart and soul had never gone into a prayer as they did now into the mere wish that he might pray.

All this time he felt himself slipping, slipping.

The tree was probably hollow to the root. Death in that horrible depth seemed certain. And who would ever think of looking for him there?

After a long while his absence would excite alarm. The woods would be searched, and his gun might be found on the log below there. But would even that give his friends a clew to his fate?

He remembered that, to an observer on the ground, there was no visible sign that the tree had an opening at the top; and who would dream of his having climbed that enormous trunk?

"Oh, why didn't I let Pete come with me?" he said despairingly, little suspecting that Pete was even then prowling in the woods, listening to hear his gun.

Still, inch by inch, he knew that he was slipping, slipping, slipping.

If he only had room to use his knees and feet! If he could clutch with his fingers some solid support! The top of the cavity was so near! Why could he not reach it?

"I must! I will!" he cried out, in a choked and stifled voice, and nerved himself for a last determined struggle.

It seemed for a minute that he was actually making progress upward; and he quickened his efforts with the energy of desperation. Then all at once something seemed to give way with his strength, and he had a sense of sliding rapidly, his fingers tearing from their hold, his nails from their sockets, and soul and body rushing down into darkness.

CHAPTER VIII

IMPRISONED

Gaspar was stunned by the fall, but not seriously hurt.

On coming to himself, he found that he was in a narrow dungeon, perhaps three feet in diameter, which smelled strongly of damp and decay. He was sitting on a soft, rotting mass of stuff, which must have served to break his fall; his legs were buried in it to the knees. He had a sense of having been terribly wrenched and jarred, with a sick and giddy feeling about the head.

The hollow was dark. He felt the rough, mouldering walls with his hands, and then looked up. A round spot of light, which did not seem very far above, showed the aperture by which he had been entrapped.

"If I had room enough to work in that narrow part up there, I could get out," he said to himself. For he had his knife in his pocket, and he believed he could cut foot-holds into the wood sufficiently solid to bear his weight.

"But it will take so long!" he thought. "I shall starve first, or smother" — for he was feeling the need of fresh air.

His mind was quickly diverted from that project by an incident. One could hardly expect to meet with an adventure at the bottom of such a tube as that; yet one happened to Gaspar.

As he was getting upon his feet, he felt something stir in the rubbish beneath him, and thought of his scarlet tanager. He thrust down his hand and seized something which was less like feathers than fur, but loosed his hold instantly on receiving a bite in the thumb. The creature thereupon scampered over his knees and darted across his shoulder and down the back of his coat, with a quick chipper which told plainly enough what sort of companion he had in his dungeon.

"A chipmunk!" he exclaimed. "Where did

the fellow go to?" For all was still again in a moment.

This trifling incident seemed important to the prisoner, and it gave him hope. He reasoned, —

"It is not the habit of chipmunks to climb trees. This one never came in at the top of the trunk; he must have a hole somewhere down here. There is probably an opening on one side as there is at the roots of most hollow trunks."

If the squirrel had his summer home there, it seemed strange that he had not run out of his door when he saw so extraordinary a visitor coming down the chimney. Some dislodged fragments of the crumbling interior must have fallen, Gaspar thought, and suddenly stopped the hole. Had the frightened animal now dived down amongst them to find his way out? If so, they had closed after him; for the prisoner could discern no glimmer of light except what came in at the top.

His eyes growing accustomed to the obscurity, he could see about all that was to be seen in that dismal place. This was very little indeed: only the dim outline of the litter beneath his feet, and the walls consumed by the slow combustion of time. He soon had out his knife, and began to chip into them, quickly striking the rings of the hard wood which supported the living branches.

"My best chance," he said, "will be to find the natural opening, if there is one." And he set himself to search for that.

After poking awhile with his feet, he was rewarded by seeing a faint gleam of light which did not come in at the top. With fresh hope and joy, he dug the rubbish away from it, and discovered a narrow, jagged slit, apparently in the angle between two branching roots.

Exploring it with his hands, he found it not more than three or four inches in breadth, and inclosed by solid folds of wood and bark. But if it did not promise immediate escape to the prisoner, it offered what was almost as welcome, — a prospect of fresh air.

"If I can breathe," he said, "I will cut my way out in time."

He burrowed still farther, throwing the rubbish in a heap behind him; but could not find that the slit enlarged as he went deeper. On the contrary, it soon grew narrower, as if the two roots — if there were two originally — were crowded together at the surface of the ground.

He could now look out and see the waning afternoon light on the dead leaves that strewed the forest floor. He had not thought that he should ever look upon that peaceful scene again; and, as he fixed his yearning eyes upon it, and drew the fresh air into his lungs, a deep sense of gratitude filled his heart, such as he had not felt in all his life before.

He could not see the pine he had climbed, nor the log on which he had left his gun; and he concluded that they must be on the opposite side of the hollow tree. The slant of the sunlight among the forest stems, and the apparent falling away of the ground in the direction of Bingham's swamp, confirmed him in this opinion.

The first thing he did, after looking out and

inhaling fresh draughts of air, was to call again for help. But now, as much of his voice as was not muffled in the tree seemed to strike down upon the earth, and to penetrate the forest no farther than when he sent it straight up into the sky.

"No use in my losing time this way!" he said, and at once set about enlarging the aperture with his knife.

The decayed part of the bark was easily scraped from the edges of the separated folds; but hard enough he found the green wood beneath. He worked away at it with right good will, however, knowing that the slightest splinter or shaving he removed, diminished by so much the barrier that kept him from liberty and home.

For home meant liberty and happiness to him now. How could he ever have scoffed at it, and nursed a moody discontent, with the blessings he enjoyed? Was it not his own fault that his father had opposed the killing of birds, and the hunting of nests and eggs, which had been so large a part of his boy life; seeing him with those low associates, in whose company he seemed to forget all the love and duty he owed his parents and friends?

He made slow progress, hurting his hand with the short-bladed knife and on the rough edges of the wood. But still he worked away, and as he worked, he thought, —

"Why was I never willing to do anything to please them, while they were always doing so much for me? Why couldn't I have seen that it was only my good they thought of when they sent me to school, and tried to have me keep better company, and be industrious, and respectful and decent! Oh, what a fool I have been!"

Yes, he had been worse than a fool; he had been headstrong in his selfish, thankless, often cruel opposition to their wishes. All this he said to himself, recalling many instances of his unworthy conduct, and longing for freedom, that he might begin life over again and redeem the past.

"What if I had died in this hole! What if I should die here now — leaving all my bad actions to be remembered! The very last thing

I did was to disobey my father and break my promise to Schoolmaster Pike; the last words I spoke to Ella were mean and unjust!"

It was growing dark; the sunlight had disappeared from the boughs and stems, and deep shadows were creeping over the solitary forest. Occasionally he ceased cutting, to look out and call, and listen. No voices answered, no footsteps approached; nor was he much disappointed, for he knew well that it was not yet time for his absence from home to excite alarm, and he was in the most unfrequented part of the woods.

It would soon be quite dark; he must make the most of what daylight was left. He expected nothing else than that he must spend the night where he was, with no near neighbors but the katydids and owls. Supperless, lonesome, oppressed by the gloom, the odors of decay, and his own terrors and regrets, the prospect was one to make a better and braver boy shudder.

"I shall work a part of the night, anyway; for when I can't see I can feel. Then, when I am tired out, I can perhaps sleep."

The night insects had struck up their monotonous notes in the darkening woods; and now a fine, incessant hum about his ears, with an occasional sting on face or hands, gave warning that a swarm of mosquitoes had found him out. He could imagine them rising, like a misty cloud, from Bingham's swamp, and dividing into two parties, one of which filed in at the aperture where he was at work, while the other poured down upon him through the opening above. They interrupted his work; how then could he hope that they would let him sleep?

Fighting the invaders with one hand, he plied his knife with the other, blistering his palm and bruising his knuckles, but determined not to give over his toil till he had made a hole that he could squeeze his body through, and get out of that terrible place. The darkness closed in upon him; he could no longer see where he thrust his blade. Patience was not one of his virtues, and he was growing desperate. The tough, green fibres would not come away fast enough, and he began to work off thicker chips, pressing and prying with the knife.

Suddenly something snapped. He uttered a cry of dismay. The knife had but one whole blade, and that had broken under his hand.

To the misery of the night that followed was now added the horrible apprehension that he might not be traced to that remote part of the woods, and that he was destined to perish in the hollow tree.

"But I can at least put my hand and some part of my clothing out of the hole," he said; "and there is my gun, which will be found some time; that will set people to looking hereabouts. But perhaps it may not be found till long after I am dead!"

He did not know that his gun had already been carried off by the prowling Pete, while he lay silent and stunned in the bottom of the hollow trunk.

CHAPTER IX

THE CLEW AND WHAT IT LED TO

Having obtained possession of the fowling-piece, Pete felt it a great grievance that he should be obliged to give it up.

"He's dead, or run away; I don't see why I can't hev it 's well 's anybody," he muttered, as he crawled into the bushes where he had concealed the gun that Sunday afternoon. "Might 's well leave it here. B'sides, ther' might be folks in the woods that 'ud see me with it."

He persuaded himself that it would be well to wait until night, at all events; in the mean time he would not go home, but live on melons, which he knew well enough where to find.

"What's b'come o' the feller, anyhow?" he said, as he crept out of the bushes again, without the gun. And that strange fascination which often attends the wrong-doer led him to wander again through the woods in the direction of Bingham's swamp.

He stopped often to look about him, and often changed his course; but invariably his feet would turn again, and his eyes look off toward the spot where he had found the gun.

At last he came in sight of the log. Then he stopped and sat down on a mossy root. After a while he went on again, not directly toward the log, but walking around it, wondering more and more how the gun ever got there, and what had become of its owner. The woods were strangely still; and he was frightened at the thought of Gaspar having shot himself and crawled away to die, perhaps in some of the hollows of the great swamp.

He stopped to pick and chew a few fresh checkerberry leaves; then, resolved not to be a coward, having looked all about again to see that nobody was in sight, he walked straight to the log.

He was still in a nervous tremor, looking first at the ground for traces of Gaspar, and then peering about in the silent woods, when all at once he heard a voice.

Where did it come from? It seemed quite near, and yet there was nobody in sight. He looked up into the trees, he looked all around again in the quiet forest, with superstitious fear — waiting quakingly until he heard the mysterious voice again, then he took to his heels.

He ran like a deer, and never stopped until, leaping over a ridge of rock, he came face to face with a man. It was Mr. Pike, the schoolmaster.

"Peter," he exclaimed, "you are the boy I was looking for!"

"Wha' d'ye want o' me?" said the breathless Pete.

"Wait, and I'll tell you," replied the master, seeing the boy inclined to avoid him and continue his flight. "What were you running for?"

"Jes' for fun — I dunno — sometimes I run, an' sometimes I don't," stammered Pete. "Isn't any law aginst a fellow's runnin', is ther'?"

"All at once he heard a voice."— Page 90.

"No," said the master sternly. "But there are laws against some other things. Don't try to get away! You are going with me, or I am going with you, whichever way it happens. But I promise to be your friend in this matter, if you'll tell me the truth."

"Truth 'bout what?"

"About Gaspar Heth."

"'Bout Gap Heth?" gasped Pete with wild eyes.

"Yes; what has become of him?"

"Dunno what's become on him; I tol' ye so last night."

"Well, then," said the master, laying hold of his ragged collar, "tell me what has become of his gun, and where you found it."

Pete glared up at him, pale and chattering with fright. He did not know how much Mr. Pike knew of the truth, and was afraid to utter a straightforward lie.

"If you won't speak, then you and I go straight to Squire Coburn's;" and Mr. Pike started to lead him off.

As Squire Coburn was the village justice,

Pete struggled and hung back; but at last he exclaimed, —

"Lemme go, an' I'll tell ye. I found the gun on a log over yender by Bingham's swamp, but Gap Heth wa'n't anywheres around, sure's I'm alive!"

"Come and show me the place," said the master.

Pete started, but presently hung back again.

"I don't want to!" he said. "That's what I was runnin' away from — his *ha'nt*."

"His what?" Mr. Pike demanded impatiently.

"His ha'nt. I heard it, jes' as plain! But I couldn't see a thing. That's what scairt me. I'm awful 'fraid o' ha'nts!"

"What do you mean by haunts? — Ghosts? Do you imagine you've heard Gaspar's ghost?"

"I know I hev!" cried Pete.

"Come along and show me the spot," said the master. "If you heard Gaspar's voice, it was Gaspar himself who called, and not his '*ha'nt*.' Come! for he must be in trouble."

Partly reassured, Pete accompanied him; but

paused again before they had gone far over the ridge.

"Ye can hear it now!" he said.

Mr. Pike listened a moment. "It is certainly Gaspar calling!" he exclaimed; and, leaving the reluctant Pete to his fears, he set out to run in the direction of the voice.

Curiosity prompted Pete to follow at a safe distance. "That's the log!" he shouted, as the master paused, not knowing which way to turn; "right afore ye!"

The voice sounded again; and Mr. Pike, standing by the log, was as much puzzled at first as Pete had been to decide whence it came. Proceeding from the hollow tree, it was like the speech of a ventriloquist; and one could imagine it almost anywhere except where it was.

But instead of running away as Pete had done, Mr. Pike called, —

"I hear you, Gaspar! where are you?"

"In the hollow tree," replied the voice. "Come around the other side."

The master had already seen far enough to

assure himself that Gaspar was not behind the tree. He now obeyed the voice, and was more disturbed than he had ever been in all his life, to see a grimy hand thrust out of an opening in the bark. If the voice was like ventriloquism, the appearance of the hand was like magic.

"Why, Gaspar!" he cried, hastening to the aperture, and seizing the hand as if to make sure of it; "how did you ever get in there?"

"I slipped in at the top, trying to get a bird."

Gaspar spoke in a stifled voice; and as he could not bring his mouth to the outer rim of the orifice, it sounded almost as if the tree itself had spoken.

Mr. Pike looked up, and the manifest impossibility of a boy's climbing that prodigious trunk added to his bewilderment. But his eyes followed the limb that curved across the top of the pine, where he saw Gaspar's cap lodged; and he required no further explanation of the mystery.

"Run as you would for your life!" he said

to the staring Pete. "Bring the nearest farmer with his axe; and get word to the Heths, if you have a chance. Say that Gaspar is found — alive — in a hollow tree!"

Pete was off again in a moment, plying those nimble legs of his.

"You can stand it ten or fifteen minutes longer," Mr. Pike said, turning again to Gaspar.

"Oh, yes," replied the prisoner in feeble and quivering accents. "After a night and a day in such a place as this, I sha'n't care for half an hour more, if you won't leave me."

"Poor fellow!" said the sympathizing master; "how you must have suffered! I won't leave you; never fear."

It is strange how the voice of pity will sometimes stir depths of the heart which agony itself could not reach. In all the wretchedness and horror of his imprisonment, Gaspar had not wept as he wept now that he was found and a friend was speaking to him consoling words.

"It hasn't been very gay in here," he said,

checking his sobs, and trying to speak cheerfully. "I'm nearly starved. And the mosquitoes — you never saw such a place for mosquitoes! But I don't care for anything now that you "— Here his sobs choked him again.

"Was there no way of getting out?" Mr. Pike inquired.

"I might have cut my way out if I hadn't broken my knife. Then, this morning, I tried climbing. The hollow is pretty large at the top and bottom, but there is a spot I couldn't get through; it's so narrow I had no chance to use my legs and arms. Then I tried digging under the trunk, but tore my fingers for nothing. There's no *under* to it. You just go right down into the hard roots."

"It's one of the most astonishing adventures I ever heard of!" exclaimed the master. "I came in sight of this place once this morning, hunting for you; but who would have ever thought of finding you in a hollow trunk? I don't wonder Pete Cheevy thought it was your ghost that called!"

"Did he?" said Gaspar with a faint laugh.

"I didn't know whether anybody would be hunting for me or not; I was afraid I mightn't be thought worth the trouble."

"What do you mean by that, Gaspar?"

"Oh, you know what I mean!" said the voice in the tree, breaking again. "I heard all your talk with my mother that first day you called at our house; and every word she said to you was true — only it wasn't half the truth! It took a night and a day in a hollow tree to bring me to my senses, and show me what a worthless wretch I have been."

It required an effort for the master to control his voice and reply, stooping to the dark aperture within which he could hear sounds of weeping, —

"It will take more than that — it will take a great many hollow trees and their lessons to convince your mother and me that you are as worthless as you think yourself now. I told her then that I was sure there was good in you which only needed to be developed."

"I know you did; I heard you," said Gaspar. "That's what made me like you. But I have treated you as I have treated all my friends, and I have got my pay for it. If I hadn't broken my promise to you about shooting birds, I shouldn't have got into this scrape. What did my folks say?"

"They haven't known what to say or think. Your disappearance has been a terrible thing to them. I believe your father concluded that you had run away; but your mother feared something worse had happened — that you had met with a fatal accident. They passed a dreadful night, as well as you, Gaspar!"

"I suppose so. I have thought of them a thousand times," murmured the boy, "knowing so well that I never was worth the least part of the trouble I have caused them."

"You may have had some reason to think so," said the master. "But I trust we shall all have reason to think very differently in the future."

"I hope so!" breathed Gaspar devoutly. "If I didn't, I should wish never to get out of this tree alive."

"The Cavity in the Big Oak." — Page 91.

CHAPTER X

"WHAT WAS LEFT OF HIM"

DURING the latter part of this conversation between the boy in the hollow tree and the man outside, the man began to look anxiously at his watch. Ten — fifteen — twenty minutes passed; and still no farmer came with his axe, and no Pete reappeared.

"Won't they ever come?" said Gaspar despairingly.

"They are a long while about it," replied the master. "If you can bear to have me leave you a few minutes, I believe I can bring somebody, or find an axe; it isn't far out of the woods on one side." He consulted his watch again, adding, "I haven't much confidence in that Pete."

"Oh, he will bring somebody, I'm certain,"

said Gaspar. "Don't go! It seems to me as if I couldn't be left alone again."

"Wait! I hear shouts!" said the master. "I believe the men Peter sent have mistaken their way and gone on the wrong side of the swamp."

He was right in his conjecture. He answered the shouts, and the men answered back. And soon the woods resounded with cries from other directions, where men and boys who had caught up the news that Pete had left on his way to the village came hurrying to see Gaspar Heth taken out of a hollow tree.

The voice of the schoolmaster, standing guard by his young friend, guided all comers to the place. And now appeared Pete himself with the gun, and his father with an axe; and the two men first named, who had lost their way, came struggling through the swamp; and that spot in the woods, which had been so silent and solitary a little while before, became a scene of surprising activity. Shouts answered shouts as other comers appeared; the oddest guesses and comments were made regarding

Gaspar's situation; and every one had to go and peep in at the narrow aperture for a glimpse of his mosquito-bitten face or his blotched and smeary hands.

"How ever did he squeeze in through that leetle hole?" said Simon Crabbe, the cobbler, who was near-sighted as well as dull-witted, and who had not yet taken in the significance of the tree's broken top. "Reminds me of a toad in a rock; but they say a toad crawls in when he's small, and grows there."

Mr. Pike explained that Gaspar was climbing after a bird, adding, "Run up the tree there, Pete, and get his cap; he will want it in a few minutes."

"After a bird!" said grim-looking old Dr. Kent. "I thought we were going to put a stop to this bird business. How is it, Mr. Pike?"

Mr. Pike appeared too busy just then to heed the question.

"Stand back," he cried, "and make room for the axes!"

The crowd drew back and the elder Cheevy

was the first to strike into the tree, making the bark and chips fly into the faces of those who remained too near. Although accounted a sort of vagabond, lazy and shiftless in his habits, he was athletic and handy with an axe; and now he had a good opportunity to show his skill. The first of the men from the swamp took a position facing him, and offered to strike in on the other side of the loop-hole he was enlarging; but old Pete warned him off.

"You'll hinder mor'n you'll help," he said. (Hack! hack!) "You jes' lay low with the rest (hack!), an' you'll see a hole 'n this 'ere shell 'n half a jiffy (hack!) that a hoss 'n cart could back out of!" (Hack! hack!) And off fell the great chips.

If it was a strange event to those looking on, waiting to see a lost boy cut out of a hollow oak, what was it to the boy himself, crouched beyond the possible reach of the axe, watching every stroke which opened wider the door of his prison and let the broad daylight in?

"That will do!" he called to the chopper. "I can get out now."

But Cheevy did not mean that he should creep out.

"You're go'n' ter walk out like a man!" he said, ending, at last, with, "Now, how's that?" as he drew back and poised his axe.

"All right!" And Gaspar leaped into the light and air of the beautiful August afternoon. "I'm much obliged to you, Mr. Cheevy! I'm much obliged to you all for coming to see what a fool I have made of myself!"

His eyes glistened and his voice was unsteady as he received the congratulations and answered the questions of friends crowding around. Suddenly he said, "Excuse me!" and, to the amazement of everybody, walked back into the tree.

"Haven't you had enough of it yet?" cried the master, looking in after him.

"Quite enough and to spare," replied Gaspar. "But there's one thing I mustn't forget." And he took down from the inner coating of the trunk something he had fastened to it with a pin.

It was his scarlet tanager, found while he

was digging in the rubbish which had treacherously flaked off and come down with him when he slipped through the narrow part of the cavity.

"I must keep this to remember this adventure by," he said with a rueful smile and a long breath, as he once more stepped out of the tree, and instinctively brushed the particles of decayed wood from the brilliant plumage. "Now, where's my gun?"

"Here 'tis; I've be'n keepin' on't fer ye!" cried young Pete Cheevy, springing forward with alacrity. "An' here's yer cap that I jes' got out o' the tree."

"Thank you very much for both, Pete!" said Gaspar earnestly, as he put on the cap; while Master Pike smiled significantly at old Pete, and old Pete winked deprecatingly at Master Pike.

Then all the young fellows, and some of the older ones, had to take turns getting into the hollow trunk, or at least putting their heads in: "Jes' so's to see," as Cobbler Crabbe expressed it, "how it must have seemed to the boy shet up there for nigh about twenty-four hours."

Meanwhile grim old Dr. Kent looked hard at the bird in Gaspar's hand, and repeated his still unanswered question to Master Pike, —

"How is it about this bird-shooting? Didn't I understand that we were all going to unite in frowning it down and putting a stop to it?"

"Yes, I believe that was the understanding," replied Master Pike.

"And didn't we agree that we'd have the first boy that should break the law prosecuted? That's what was publicly given out as a notice and warning to all; wasn't it?"

The schoolmaster nodded a reluctant assent.

"Well," said the doctor with an emphasis meant to clinch his argument, "I don't want to mar the good feeling of a time like this. Gaspar has been rescued from a bad fix, and I'm glad of it. But let's be consistent; don't let us be respecters of persons. His father's a minister, and a man we all respect, and a good friend of mine besides; but if his son — and I'd say the same if he were mine — is guilty of breaking the law we've pledged ourselves to see enforced, I don't see but that we ought to make an example of him. It will be a good beginning."

"Your remarks are just," replied Master Pike. "And though I think Gaspar has been punished enough for a good many faults besides bird-shooting, I shouldn't object to seeing him prosecuted and fined if he had broken the law in this case. But he has not."

"Not broken the law?" cried the grim-featured doctor, "with that dead bird in his hand?"

All eyes turned upon Gaspar, who was about to speak, when the master forestalled him.

"No, doctor; and a prosecution in this case wouldn't hold water. Gaspar is an ornithologist, or is going to be one; and he has a certificate from the Natural History Society which allows him to take birds for scientific purposes. Here it is."

He took from his pocket the paper which he was to have given Gaspar the night before.

"It is dated, you see, two days ago; so that the shooting of this tanager is a case exempt from the action of the law."

"To be sure! to be sure!" said the doctor; while Gaspar stared with mingled feelings of astonishment and gratitude.

"You had it for me all the time, and to think I didn't know it!" he said to Master Pike on their way out of the woods. "You are too easy with me; for I really deserved to forfeit it for breaking my promise."

"I think," replied the master indulgently, "you will keep your promises better in future."

He had good reason for such a belief; thenceforward his influence over his pupil was complete.

Before they emerged from the woods, they were met by Minister Heth, who had heard the news, and was hastening to the scene of the rescue. At sight of his son, saved from a horrible fate, haggard, famished, insect-bitten, with soiled and blood-smeared hands, he forgot all his resentment, and, like waters from a broken dam, his paternal love gushed forth.

All he said, however, was simply,— in a voice and with features which a strong will controlled, —

"Gaspar! is it you at last?"

"Yes, what there is left of me!" replied Gaspar with the same self-control. "How's mother?"

"She will be better for seeing you, Gaspar!" said the minister, his resolute voice beginning to quaver and give way. "Come, my boy!"

What was left of him, after twenty-four hours in a dungeon with remorse and fear and starvation and mosquitoes — Gaspar might well say that. He had lost something which he could well spare; and what was left was the better part of him, as his conduct thenceforward, up to this date, has proven.

He has not yet chosen the career by which he is to earn his living; but he is preparing himself for usefulness by laying a broad foundation of knowledge; and whatever work he may do in the world, he means that the pursuit in which he still delights — the study of birds — shall be his recreation.

He has learned to stuff and mount his specimens; and if you visit the family, you will see on the parlor mantel-piece a beautiful sample of his work, which, from the associations connected with it, has an especial value in the eyes of his friends.

It is the Scarlet Tanager.

GRANDMOTHER'S GOLD BEADS

CHAPTER I

APPEARANCES were certainly very strong against John Henry. His legs were seen just disappearing through a hole in the fence, when Mrs. Chary heard the baby scream and ran out.

Baby was in the hammock, where she had been very well contented for the last half-hour. She had her doll in her arms, and grandmother's gold beads on her neck; and then John Henry had crawled through the fence to pay her a little visit.

John Henry Fay was a peculiar boy; "girl-boy" his mates called him with some contempt. He dreaded their rough sports; and if he could get away from them, and go and play with little girls somewhere, he was happy. Worse than that, he was even fond of babies! To youngsters of his own age, that seemed extraordinary baseness in a boy of thirteen.

Well, Baby screamed, and mamma ran out, and there were John Henry's legs going through the fence, and there was the doll, which had just fallen out of the hammock; but where, oh, where, were the gold beads?

Grandmother had herself put them on Baby's neck when she left her in the hammock. The hammock was hung between two apple-trees in the back yard, where nobody could approach it without being seen; and Baby had not been out of mamma's sight a minute.

Mrs. Chary had picked up the doll before she noticed that the beads were missing. Then you should have heard her cry out.

"Why, Baby, where are grandma's beads?"

Baby hugged her doll, stopped screaming, and answered in a dazed sort of way, after the question had been twice repeated, — "Henny, — bead — gone!"

"John Henry! Did he take your beads?" said mamma, very much excited.

Baby turned her large blue eyes towards the

hole in the fence, and said again, with a vague, wondering look, " Henny, bead! Gamma, bead, too bad!"

Grandmother had by this time come out, and so had the girls; and in the midst of the excitement that followed, Chuck Chary came home.

Chuck's real name was Washington. But Washington is a rather long and strong name for a small boy; and one can hardly blame his mates for shortening it. But how they ever made *Chuck* out of it is more than I know.

Chuck he was, however. Some boy, in a moment of inspiration, had given him that nickname; and Chuck Chary suited well that short, stout body and impetuous, plucky spirit of his.

Chuck was fifteen. But when he heard the story of the beads and the disappearing legs, he thought he was a man grown; he stretched himself up, and swelled and strutted and crowed, so much like the cockerel in the back yard, that I am sure he would have got well laughed at by his sisters, if the business on hand had not been so serious.

Grandmother had had her beads fifty years;

and she was going to give them to Mary Jane, if she ever got through with them. The girls regarded them with great veneration; and it was always considered a treat when the old lady brought them out and put them on one of their necks of an afternoon.

Chuck had never cared so much about them; but he displayed an almost too fiery zeal now that he heard of their loss and could do something for their recovery.

"You can't find 'em, hunting there on the ground," he called out, shaking his head in a warlike way, and looking awfully fierce. "May as well give that up first as last."

"Wal, I hain't much hope on't," said grandmother, bending her poor old rheumatic back as she went stooping under the trees; "but I thought I might as well be sure."

The grass grew very sparsely there, even in the spring; and now in September it was all shrivelled up and worn away for a good space around the hammock. Any gold beads which Baby might have scattered around there must easily have been seen.

"I never lost but three of them string of beads before, and two on 'em I found again; and I've had 'em goin' on fifty year!" said grandmother, dropping off her spectacles as she looked, and then dropping her ball of yarn as she stooped to pick up her glasses.

"Well, you'll find these again, or else somebody'll get a broken neck!" said Chuck, with terrible significance.

"Why, Chuck!" said Mary Jane, "what *somebody* do you mean?"

"I mean that sneaking John Henry Fay!" Chuck exclaimed. "Of course he's got 'em!"

There could be little doubt about that. But Mrs. Chary entreated her boy to be calm. "The Fays are our neighbors," she said; "and I beg of you not to say or do anything that will make trouble between us!"

"*I?*" Chuck retorted scornfully. "It's that sly, meeching gal-boy of a John Henry that's made the trouble. Think I'm going to let him creep in here through the fence and carry off gran'ma's gold beads, and sit down and fold my hands and hold my tongue and grin at it, just because they're our neighbors?"

"But he's young! It must have been a great temptation; and I can't believe he has taken them, meaning to steal them," Mrs. Chary insisted.

"Well, then he'll have a chance to explain himself and give 'em up," said Chuck. "Anyhow, I'm going to speak to him about it."

His face was flushed and his look was still fierce; and good Mrs. Chary implored, even commanded, him to wait a while.

"There he is now," cried Chuck, "coming out of the barn. He's been to hide the beads, I'll bet a dollar. I'm going for that John Henry!"

He ran to the fence spite of all his mother could say; and in a moment more had tumbled himself over upon the premises of neighbor Fay.

When John Henry saw this threatening movement, he turned and started to run away.

"Look here, gal-boy!" cried Chuck, speeding after him on those short, stout legs of his.

"What do you want?" he gasped out. — Page 117.

The timid one stopped and turned again, with a pale and troubled face, which appeared to the other certain evidence of his guilt. "What do you want?" he gasped out, as Chuck blustered up to him.

"Oh, yes!" scoffed the Chary boy; "what *do* I want? That's a pretty question for you to ask! Hand over now, before I make you!"

"I don't know what you mean," said John Henry, white and trembling.

"Don't, hey? Then I'll tell you. I want those gold beads!" and Chuck held out his hand with a determined look.

"What gold beads?" said John Henry, getting his breath by this time and a little courage with it.

"Oh, you don't know anything about 'em, do you?"

"I'm sure I don't!"

"You haven't been through that hole in the fence this afternoon, hey?" said Chuck with grim sarcasm.

"Yes, I have!" John Henry declared, staring with large eyes.

"Oh, you have, have ye? I thought maybe you'd deny that, too! Went to call on our baby, did ye? A manly fellow you are! Why don't you crawl through the fence when I'm there sometimes?"

"Because I don't like to play with you, you're so rough."

"Rough, am I?" returned Chuck angrily. "I'll show you whether I'm rough or not, if you don't hand me over those beads this minute." And he grasped John Henry by the shoulder.

CHAPTER II

By this time Mrs. Fay, hearing high words in the barn-yard, and seeing the Chary boy in the very act of laying violent hands on *her* boy, hastened to the spot.

She was a woman of the kindest heart and the gentlest manners. But behind all she had a spirit which could be greatly roused, as such people often have. And she was a mother, — all the more sensitively fond of her John Henry on account of his too amiable and girlish disposition.

"What is this?" she demanded, putting one hand on her son's arm and the other on that of his assailant. "My son, what is this all about?"

"I don't know. Sure as I live and breathe," John Henry exclaimed, "I don't know anything what he means, or what he wants!"

"Take your hand off from him and tell me!"

said Mrs. Fay sharply to Chuck. "If you come into our yard to abuse our boy, I want to know what it is for."

"You may know," cried Chuck insolently; but he took his hand from John Henry's collar, and stood back a little. "Your boy has been in *our yard*, and taken gran'ma's gold beads from Baby's neck, and I've come for 'em and I'm going to have 'em — that's all! That's what it's for."

Hearing this charge, and seeing the sturdy little Chuck standing before her, so red and wrathful, so puffed with importance, and so impudent, the mother of John Henry was quite bewildered for a moment. She looked from one boy to the other, while John Henry exclaimed, "I don't know anything about the gold beads! I haven't touched them, and I haven't seen them; I hope to die if I have!"

"He has!" struck in Chuck stormfully. "They were on Baby's neck in the hammock, and nobody else went near her there, and he sneaked in through the fence to play with her, and stole 'em and ran soon as ever he saw mother coming out."

"Washington Chary," cried Mrs. Fay, bursting with indignation, "that's all an impudent falsehood! The idea of *you* accusing *John Henry* of stealing!"

"Oh, *I steal* do I?" sputtered Chuck with fresh fury.

"As to that, I'm not quite so ready to charge boys with stealing as *some folks* are," said Mrs. Fay. "But everybody knows that you're a rough, ill-mannered fellow, and far more likely to get into any sort of mischief than ever my John Henry was."

Thereupon Chuck's mother called to him from the fence, "Come away, my son! I told you not to go there!"

"Well," cried Chuck in a high voice, "I'm glad I came, for I've found out what she thinks of me. I'm a liar and a ruffian, and her pretty little gal-boy is an angel!"

"What do you say my son lies about?" Mrs. Chary demanded of Mrs. Fay.

"He says my boy has stolen your gold beads; and when anybody charges such a thing as that on my John Henry, I characterize it as it deserves," Mrs. Fay said to Mrs. Chary.

"I don't see the need of your getting into a temper about it," Mrs. Chary replied, herself in a pretty high temper by this time. "You might at least be willing to hear the simple facts in the case."

"And do *you* accuse my John Henry?" began Mrs. Fay. "Do you, Mrs. Chary, dare to stand there at the boundary fence and say my John Henry is a thief?"

"I haven't said that," Mrs. Chary replied. "But I *do* say that the beads were on Baby's neck when she was left in the hammock; that when I went to her, they were gone, and that nobody under the sun had been near her but your John Henry. When he saw me, he ran; and when I asked Baby about the beads, she pointed after him and said, '*Henry got beads!*'"

"And because the beads are lost, and a baby eighteen months old says John Henry took them, he is convicted as a thief!" said Mrs. Fay. "I'm astonished at you, Mrs. Chary! I thought it bad enough when your boy came over here with his impudence; but now, to hear you uphold him, and use such language, — it is shameful!"

"That I have occasion to use such language — that is the shameful part of it," retorted Mrs. Chary. "I'm very sorry if it hurts your feelings; but I've looked into the matter thoroughly; and there's no doubt in my mind where those beads went to. Come home, Washington!"

The two households furnished several spectators to this lively scene. Among the rest, Russell Fay — an elder brother of the girl-boy — had come home in time to hear a portion of the dialogue between the two women, and to learn from John Henry what it was all about.

He was a tall fellow of seventeen, and he did not share at all his brother's meek disposition. The quarrel now raged between him and Chuck, who retreated backwards to the fence, all the time daring Russell to strike him, and taunting him with his size.

"Well," jeered Russell, as Chuck finally got

over the fence, "you'd *better* get on your own ground! And don't you let me see you on our premises again, unless you want a thrashing!"

"It'll take more than you to give it to me, Russ Fay, big as you are!" returned Chuck. "And let me advise you to keep that little thieving brother of yours at home; don't let me hear of his crawling through the fence again!"

"You're a pretty fellow to talk!" said Russ. "Why don't you keep your hens at home? There's your rooster in our garden now! I've stood that nonsense long enough, and now I'm going to kill him!"

"Kill him if you want to!" cried Chuck defiantly.

Thereupon, Russ, taking Chuck at his word, turned his fury towards the unfortunate fowl. A too-convenient club came to his hand. It was hurled with force and precision. The cackling and fluttering of the escaping cockerel suddenly ceased; and presently his dead carcass was hurled ignominiously over the fence into the Charys' yard.

Mr. Chary himself arrived in time to see that, and to hear Russell's jubilant yell: "There's your old rooster! He won't trouble us again!"

To say that Mr. Chary was astonished would be using a mild term. He was an irritable little man; and when he heard Chuck's side of the story, he flew into a violent passion.

He was walking up and down in the back yard denouncing Russell's conduct in a high-keyed voice, and threatening to have the thief who had stolen the beads taken up, no matter whose boy he was, when a tall, square-shouldered, mealy-looking man appeared on the other side of the fence.

John Henry, frightened at the tumult of which he was the cause, had been to fetch his father from the mill near by. It was Mr. Fay, in his miller's hat and frock, with whited hair and whiskers, who now approached the boundary.

"Oh, dear!" exclaimed poor Mrs. Chary, looking out from the kitchen, into which she had retired in great agitation, "now the men are going to take up the quarrel!"

"Don't let 'em!" said Mary Jane, running out to Chuck. "Mr. Fay is big enough to eat father up, and he looks as if he would!"

"You just go back into the house, and mind your own business! You're nothing but a girl!" said Chuck. "Anybody that eats father has got to eat me!"

And the puffy little red-faced chap looked as if he were quite ready, for his part, to have the eating begin.

CHAPTER III

The square-shouldered miller was a quiet sort of man. But after hearing John Henry's side of the story, and catching some of Mr. Chary's violent words, he was very much incensed.

"Neighbor Chary," he said, standing breast-high above the fence, "it seems to me that's foolish sort of talk you're indulging in!"

"Foolish or not, Neighbor Fay, it's true!" Neighbor Chary answered back, blustering up to the fence. "I didn't mean it for your ears; but I don't care; you may as well know what I think."

Neighbor Fay looked as if he would like to reach over and catch the elder Chary with one hand and Chuck with the other, and knock their belligerent heads together. But he didn't.

"You've always passed for tolerably decent

neighbors till now," he said, restraining his wrath; "but, by George, I believe you're all crazy!"

"If there's any more craziness our side of the fence than there is yours, we're a pretty looney lot, that's all!" cried Neighbor Chary. "Look at that dead rooster!"

"I've spoken to you about your hens before, and you might keep 'em shut up, as I do mine," said Neighbor Fay. "But I don't think Russell meant to kill it."

"Didn't, hey?" retorted Neighbor Chary. "Ask my folks! Ask him!"

Russ stood by and grinned maliciously. "Yes, I did mean to kill it!" he avowed.

"Well, if he did," said Neighbor Fay, "it's because your boy provoked him to it."

"If my boy did any provoking, it was because *he* was provoked," Neighbor Chary retorted. "There's a string of gold beads missing on our side of the fence, and we know who has got 'em."

Then the two men "had it hot and heavy," as Chuck said afterwards. They both became so angry that if they did not actually come to blows, it was because the fence was between them.

At length Neighbor Fay turned to walk towards his house. Neighbor Chary walked off in the other direction, but stopped suddenly and turned to Chuck. "Take that rooster and throw it over the fence!" he exclaimed. "They can have it, if it's any satisfaction to them."

Chuck was only too glad to obey; and once more the bright-feathered cockerel described a rainbow arch over the boundary.

Russ did not wait to be told by his father to fling it back again. As Chuck was following his father to the house, down tumbled the carcass in a rumpled heap at his feet.

There's no knowing how long this game might have been kept up, if grandmother had not now interposed with milder counsels. In her eyes a fowl was a fowl; and though the beads were lost and everybody was in a passion, she saw no reason why a nice fricassee should be sacrificed. So she made Mary Jane run and get the bird again, and bring it to her in the woodshed.

As soon as the battle of words was over, the worthy miller began to regret his part in it.

"I am so sorry! so sorry!" said Mrs. Fay in great distress.

"So am I," said the miller. "I wouldn't have had such a thing happen with a neighbor for a thousand dollars! But," he added, "I am sure John Henry is innocent."

"Oh, certainly!" said Mrs. Fay. "It was an outrageous charge; and that Chary boy's impudence to me was really intolerable. I never would have supposed his mother would bear him out in it. But, after all, they are our neighbors."

"And they really think John Henry took the beads," returned her husband. "It is an outrage, as you say; but evidently they are sincere. John Henry!" he called.

The boy came, agitated and tearful.

"Are you sure," said his father, "that you know nothing about the beads?"

John Henry began to sob. Was it from a

sense of guilt, or of grief because, after all his denials, his father could ask him such a question?

"I just went over to see the baby a little while," he explained as soon as he could speak. "And I didn't see any beads at all. Just as I was coming away — for I was afraid Chuck would come home and find me there — Baby dropped her doll out of the hammock, and screamed for me to come and pick it up for her. I was going to, but I saw her mother come out, and so I crawled through the fence. And that's all I know about it."

"There! don't talk about it any more!" the mother pleaded. "I am sure our boy is truthful."

"I'm bound to believe him," Mr. Fay said. "But it's very strange; and I'd give something to know what ever became of those beads."

"Chuck said I'd been hiding 'em in the barn," said John Henry.

At that moment Russ burst abruptly into the house, looking more excited than ever. "See what I found down in the straw by the stable!" he exclaimed; and he held up to view an object, the sight of which filled his parents with consternation.

"By *our* stable?" Mr. Fay demanded.

"Yes, by our stable," said Russ. "Has anybody been in our yard to-day? Anybody but Chuck, I mean, and John Henry?"

"Chuck didn't go near the barn," poor Mr. Fay faltered, overcome by sudden heart-sickness. "And John Henry"—

He turned and looked at his favorite son. He stood speechless, his eyes wide with dismay, his face white as a sheet.

Meanwhile, Neighbor Chary also had had time to cool down a little; and he began to wonder whether his side of the fence were at all to blame.

But the main facts remained. Baby had the beads in the hammock. Nobody went near her there but John Henry. The yard had been thoroughly searched for them, and every article of her clothing taken off and examined. There was but one rational theory to account for their disappearance.

"THE BEADS! MY GOLD BEADS!"—Page 133.

"I wouldn't have had this trouble with the Fays for a bushel of gold beads!" Mr. Chary exclaimed. "We may have been hasty; but there can be no kind of doubt but what that sly little John Henry took 'em."

At that moment grandmother was heard to utter cries of amazement; and presently she came rushing in from the shed, with her spectacles in one hand and something precious clasped in the other.

"What is it, grandma?" cried Chuck.

"The beads! my gold beads!" she exclaimed with hysterical glee.

"Have the Fays flung 'em over the fence, as they did the rooster?" Chuck demanded.

"Yes — they did — I'll tell you — only let me get my breath a little!" and grandmother sank down upon a chair, utterly unable to speak another word for about a minute.

CHAPTER IV

During that minute we will go back to the Fays, and the discovery which had given them such a shock. The thing Russell brought in from the barn-yard was nothing more nor less than three gold beads hanging to a broken string.

"How did they ever get there by our stable? And where's the rest of 'em? That's what I want to know!" said the elder brother, who was also beginning to think he had been hasty in dealing with their neighbor's son, and more especially with their neighbor's rooster.

The miller heaved a great sigh, "Look here, John Henry!" he said, in a quivering voice, which he tried to keep steady, while he took the trembling boy by the arm. "Now, I want to know all about this matter. Stop crying, and try to think. Did you drop that string by the stable when you saw Chuck Chary coming over the fence?"

In answer to this terrible question, John Henry could do nothing but sob. His father heaved another big sigh. His mother, with the most distressful anxiety, waited for him to speak.

"It's an awful thing that has happened," said the miller. "But we *must* know the truth. To do wrong is bad enough; but it is worse still to lie about it."

"O my son!" broke in Mrs. Fay, "do speak and clear up this dreadful doubt. You are the only person, I am sure, that has passed from the Chary place to ours, to go anywhere near our stable to-day. Still, I don't believe you meant to steal the beads. Do speak and tell us again that you did not!"

The boy tried indeed to speak, but instead of words, there came only a suffocating gasp; and the next moment he fell upon the floor in a sort of paroxysm.

Both his parents were astonished; and his

fault — if he had really committed a fault — was forgotten in their alarm for his safety.

He was an extremely tender-hearted, sensitive child; and how did they know that Russell's discovery, and these questions — showing that there was overwhelming evidence of his guilt, which they were forced to believe — had not thrown him into this convulsion, even though he were innocent?

The grandmother of the Chary household had by this time got her breath again. The beads *she* had discovered were detached from the string, and when Chuck saw them in her hand, he exclaimed, "But the Fays couldn't have flung *them* over the fence, for how could you find 'em?"

"They did!" she replied, still a little hysterical. "But they didn't know it. They flung 'em over when they did the rooster. I found 'em in his crop!"

"In his crop!" ejaculated Chuck.

"Impossible!" said his father.

"And we've been accusing that poor little John Henry!" added Mary Jane. "For my part, I *knew* he couldn't have taken them. He isn't that style of boy."

"If you knew it, why didn't you say so?" demanded her brother. "We *all* thought John Henry took 'em, and we had *reason* to think so!" he declared.

"Yes," said his father. "For who ever heard of hens eating gold beads? It beats everything I ever heard of in all my life!"

"Baby must have broken the string, and then the rooster must have picked them up for corn," said Mrs. Chary.

"Or gravel," added her husband.

"Queer kind of gravel, I should say!" commented Chuck.

"Why, Baby!" said grandmother, reproachfully, "why did you say John Henry took the beads?"

"Henny — bead — *henny!*" was the emphatic response.

"Oh!" cried Mary Jane, "she don't mean John Henry at all. She means the *hens* took the beads."

The baby crowed with satisfaction; and

there was general rejoicing over the solution of the mystery.

But twelve of the beads had been found in the cockerel's crop; but they were enough to show where the rest had probably gone. And now Mary Jane remembered that she had that afternoon seen the hens quite excited over something near the boundary fence.

"Why didn't you say that, too, about an hour ago?" Chuck demanded. "I think *you're* the one that's to blame for all this fuss."

"I shouldn't think *you* would go to blaming anybody else, when the fuss, as you call it, is all owing to *you!*" exclaimed Mary Jane with spirit. "Mother *told* you not to go near the Fays, but you *would go!*"

"There, there, Mary Jane!" said the father. "I think we're all to blame, in one sense. Now, what we're going to do, I don't know."

"Kill the rest of the flock, and pick the gold beads out of their crops, I suppose. Shall I go at 'em now?" said the impetuous Chuck.

"No, wait till they go to roost. But I didn't mean that. We've got a heavy quarrel with our neighbors on our hands, and we're responsible for it; that's what bothers me now," said Mr. Chary despondently.

"I don't see any other way for us," replied the wife, "but the honorable one."

"What's that?"

"Why, to go right over to them, and tell them the beads are found, that we were in the wrong, and apologize."

"That is pretty humble pie for us to eat," said Mr. Chary. "Who'll go? You?"

"I think *you* ought to go," replied his wife.

John Henry had come out of his paroxysm by this time, but his parents were so afraid of sending him into another, that they forbore to ask him any more exciting questions. They left him lying on the lounge in the sitting-room, and went to talk over the matter by themselves in the kitchen.

"I don't believe yet that he ever meant to steal the beads," said his mother. "But I hold to fair and upright dealings with neighbors; and I think we must let the Charys know what we have found."

"I suppose so," the miller reluctantly admitted; "though that will seem almost like confessing that our boy is guilty."

"I don't confess anything of the kind," said Mrs. Fay. "But whatever it seems like, it is something they ought to know."

"And it will be showing 'em good-will and honest intentions," suggested the miller.

CHAPTER V

Russ, meanwhile, had been searching for more beads, but without success. At length Mr. Fay took the three that had been found, and set out to take them around by the front way to his neighbors.

As he went out through the gate into the street, he saw Mr. Chary also going out at *his* gate, and coming towards him. The two men met about half-way, both looking very much ashamed.

Mr. Chary was quite surprised to see his neighbor approach him so amicably; and the miller could hardly believe that the peaceable little man was the same who had blustered up at him so furiously at the garden fence an hour ago.

"I have come to beg your pardon, Neighbor Fay," Neighbor Chary said.

Neighbor Fay was still more surprised.

"Really," he began, "*I* have to beg *your* pardon, Neighbor Chary."

"No, no, excuse me!" said Neighbor Chary.

"Yes, yes, I insist!" said Neighbor Fay. "My boy ought not to have killed your rooster!"

"I'm plaguy glad he did!" cried Neighbor Chary. "My hens shall never trouble you any more. I am going to have 'em all killed to-night."

"Not on *my* account, I beg of you," said Neighbor Fay. "The little damage they do at this season of the year isn't worth speaking of; and I give you credit for having always kept them shut up in spring and early summer. I was very hasty in what I said, and I was very wrong."

This astonishing mildness and condescension on the part of Neighbor Fay made Neighbor Chary's explanation unexpectedly easy to him. "It was *our* side of the fence that was hasty, Neighbor Fay, I frankly confess. But we thought — we *thought* — we had reason. Those beads" —

"Yes, those beads!" said the miller. "I understand fully your position, and I can't blame you for having some suspicions of our John Henry. Circumstances seemed really to be against him, but"—

"Why, no!" interrupted Neighbor Chary. "Don't think, Neighbor Fay, that *any* circumstances would make me, in my sober judgment, doubt for a moment the honesty of one of your boys."

"It is a great relief to hear you say that," said Neighbor Fay. "It makes it all the more gratifying to me to tell you that the beads"—

"The beads," again Neighbor Chary interrupted, "why, the beads—as I came to tell you—the beads are found."

Even as he said this, he looked into the miller's outstretched hand.

"Found! How?" said Neighbor Fay.

"Where did you get *those*?" cried Neighbor Chary.

The two men spoke at once, and looked at each other in astonishment.

Explanations quickly followed, and it was

concluded that the hens, in fighting for the beads, had carried the string with three attached into Mr. Fay's barn-yard, and dropped it by the stable.

The men then separated, each hastening home with the good news of peace and reconciliation.

To learn that all suspicion was removed from her darling boy was glad tidings indeed to Mrs. Fay, after the misery she had just gone through.

"But why *did* you act so when I asked you a few questions?" Mr. Fay inquired of John Henry.

"Oh, to *think* you and mamma could believe I would steal! It just about killed me!" replied the boy; and he almost went into another nervous spasm at the recollection.

His mother soothed him; and the happiness which burst upon the family after the storm filled his heart also with its gracious sunshine.

At that moment Mr. Chary was saying solemnly, "This teaches us, my son, not to be hasty and passionate in our words or dealings with those we think have wronged us;" which moral conclusion from lips that had lately been hot with wrath caused a general smile to pervade the Chary household.

"But it does good, sometimes, for a feller to get mad," said Chuck.

"How so, my son?" asked his father.

"Why, don't you see?" replied the boy. "We shouldn't ever have known what took the beads if I hadn't got mad, and made Russ get mad and kill the rooster."

That evening there was a terrible squawking in the Chary hen-house; and before nine o'clock Chuck announced to Russ over the fence that all the beads had been found except two. Those never turned up again, having probably been lost among the grass or in the straw.

HILE HARDACK'S NEWFOUND-
LAND PUP

THERE was a tribe of those Hardack boys (said Uncle Jed). There was Reub, and Tom, and Hile, and Philete, and I don't know how many more, all the way down to Cub, the baby; not a girl amongst them.

Perhaps that's what made them so rough. Girls are the sweetening in the family cup, which is apt to be rather bitter-tasting without them. They were plucky boys, but mean. Mercy on them, *weren't* they mean! I don't know that they would really steal, but they'd do the next thing to it; even cheat each other, and give each other away whenever there was a cent to be made by it. You've seen a penful of pigs push and root each other out, every one bent on getting the best chance? Well, that was the Hardack style. Every one for himself, and the crowd against everybody else.

Hile — his name was Jehile or Jehiel — was one of the sharpest of them; and one summer he took a notion that he could make money by buying a Newfoundland pup when he was small, and selling him when he was full grown. The Goldin boys had a fine litter of Newfoundlands that year: five of them, all just alike. Beautiful little fellows they were.

Well, Hile went over to Goldin's one day, and bargained for one of the pups; for which he agreed to give three days' work, husking corn. As it was getting big enough to lap milk out of a saucer, they supposed he would take it away in a day or two. But that wasn't Hile Hardack's idea. He kept making one excuse or another for leaving the pup at Goldin's, for every day he was getting the pup's board for nothing, and making so much out of his growth.

But one day March Goldin met him, and says he, "Look here, Hile, how about that pup? Ye goin' to take him or not?"

"Course I'm goin' to take him," says Hile. "Wha' che talkin' 'bout?"

"His stock's risin', an' ye know it," says March. "He's wuth more'n five days' works now, such days' works as you give, an' bime-by he'll be wuth ten. We're goin' to clear out all them pups within a week, an' if you want your'n, you must take him to-day."

"Won't to-morrer do?" says Jehile, anxious to squeeze one more day's board out of the Goldins.

"Wal, to-morrer, 't the very latest," says March, who was a good-natured fellow — they were all good-natured boys, the Goldins. "Mind!" says he; "I don't keep him an hour longer for ye 'an to-morrer noon."

"I don't see how I can git over much afore evenin'," says Jehile.

"Pleg on ye!" says March, who couldn't help laughing at the fellow's meanness. "Evenin' then! But not later'n sundown."

So, just at sunset the next day, Hile went over and made his choice among the pups; they were all so near alike you could hardly tell them apart; big enough by that time to caper around the barn floor, and even play in the yard. Hile was tickled to see them grown so, and he hurried home with his pup, and slipped him into a bag for safe keeping while he went in to eat his supper. The pup whined and scratched and scrambled a good deal in the bag at first, and Hile had to draw the strings pretty tight to keep him from escaping. Then he left him, and went in to his supper of brown bread and cold baked beans, and never thought about the little Newfoundland tied up in the sack, till he went out to show him to Philete, and to boast of his bargain.

"I can take him to town an' sell him for ten or fifteen dollars in the spring — mabby twenty-five," he was saying, as he loosed the strings. "Guess he's asleep. What makes him keep so awful still?"

"Guess he's dead," said Philete.

And dead he was; smothered in the bag. Hile was angry enough. He poked the pup over, and tried to coax life back into him, but 'twas no use. First he cried, and then he scolded, and blamed the pup for dying, and the Goldin boys for selling a dog that couldn't stand being tied up just a few minutes in a sack where he couldn't breathe. As if anybody was responsible but his own selfish, ignorant self!

"'Tain't my fault," said he. "How'd I know he'd up an' die in the bag? An' it sha'n't be my loss, nuther. Goldin boys have got four live pups left, an' I hain't got nary one but a dead one!"

Then he began to study how he could escape his loss. In a minute or two he said to Philete, "I'll give ye my ol' jackknife if you'll hold your tongue 'bout his dyin' in the bag, an' do what I want of ye to-night."

"What's that?" said Philete, who wanted the knife, of course, as any boy would.

"We'll carry him back, an' swap him for a live one. I'm 'titled to a live one, ain't I? Didn't bargain for no dead pup, did I?"

"But the boys won't trade," says Philete.

"They needn't know about it," says Hile. "We can git into the barn an' make the swap;

an' I'll have the live pup I bargained for, an' they'll think one o' their'n died in the night. I'll give ye my ol' knife jes' to go with me an' keep watch, an' help a little."

"Oh, I do'wanter," says Philete, though he was really only holding off so as to make better terms. Hile agreed to throw in twenty butternuts. Philete wanted thirty, but finally closed the bargain at twenty-five. Then about nine o'clock they took the dead puppy in a covered basket, and stole slyly around through the fields to Goldin's old barn.

They had no trouble getting in, for the Goldins kept nothing there which they thought anybody would steal, and it wasn't locked. Hile placed his dead pup back in the bed with the live ones, and put a live one into his basket. It was a clear night, and the moon shone through cracks in the boards, and through a little opening in the door, where Philete was keeping watch, when all at once Philete whispered,—

"Somebody comin'! somebody comin'!"

Hile ran and looked, and sure enough there were three big boys with a lantern, coming along the path from the house. He hurried to put the live pup back into the nest. But that wouldn't do, unless he took out the dead one again, and he was afraid he couldn't do that without having more trouble with the mother Newfoundland than he cared for just then; she had snarled when he disturbed them in the first place. So he rushed back to the door, and there were the boys with the lantern not more than two rods off, chatting and laughing. Two of them were Goldins, March and Tobe, and the other was a friend of theirs, Sim Colby, that they were taking out to show the famous pups.

There was no getting out of the barn without being seen, and the only thing for the Hardacks to do was to face the boys, or hide. Hiding was more in their line. Philete dropped down on the floor and crawled under an old sleigh in the corner. Hile only waited to pull the door to and slip the wooden latch softly, and then down he dropped after Philete.

The Goldin boys lingered for a moment at the door, and stood talking. This gave the Hardacks a chance, or they would have been detected immediately. There was a lot of rubbish stowed under the sleigh, and it didn't leave them any too much room to stow away their bodies. After Philete had crawled in, Hile backed in after him, but found his head sticking out like a mud-turtle's from his shell.

"Git along further!" he says to Philete, giving him a kick.

"I can't," whispered Philete. "Thunderation! What have I got into?" says he.

"What is it?" says Hile, still kicking and crowding.

"Hens'-nests," says Philete. "I'm wallerin' in eggs!"

"Waller in 'em!" says Hile. "Crawl, crawl, I tell ye!"

"Stop yer kickin', or I'll kick back," says Philete. "A weasel couldn't crawl in this place. Oh, what a muss!" says he. "It's too late to suck 'em," referring to the eggs.

He said afterward that if he had been a boat he could "have jest sailed in whites and yelks. As 'twas, he only jest got aground an' stuck."

Hile stopped kicking, for he knew Philete

"The Pup ran back into the Barn." — Page 157.

had a pair of heels that might send him, like a shot from a cannon, right out from under the sleigh into the breastworks of the boys entering the barn. He stowed himself in as close quarters as he could, and grabbed some straw to hide the part of him the sleigh didn't, and tucked the basket with the pup in it, under his arm, and held his breath, while March and Tobe came sauntering in, with their friend Sim and the lantern.

They were talking about dogs. The Goldin boys showed the pups, and bragged about them. The lantern shone far enough under the sleigh to have exposed Philete stranded in hens'-nests, and Hile behind him, hugging the basket and clutching at the straw, if they had been looking for interlopers among the rubbish. All at once Tobe said, —

"One o' them pups is dead!"

"How in time did that hap'n?" says March. Then they took out Hile's pup, and examined him, and wondered over him, thinking first of one thing and then of another that might have happened to him, but never guessing the secret, nor once suspecting that it was the one they had sold. All the time Hile was so tickled over their wonderment and his own cunning in playing the trick, that he could hardly help spoiling it by laughing aloud.

His shaking with silent laughter or something else stirred up the pup in his basket. The little fellow had seemed to go to sleep, when he was first put in; but now he began to turn and scratch, and whine, finding the air close. Perhaps he feared the fate of his predecessor in the bag. That rumpus took the fun out of Jehile. There was no stopping it unless he killed the pup, and he'd have done that quickly enough if he could have got his hands on his muzzle and strangled him without noise. At last, the little unreasonable cur began to yelp.

" Where — what's that ? " says March. " Hark ! "

" It's a puppy ! " said Tobe. " He's under the barn-floor ! "

" No; he's somewhere outside," said Sim Colby.

For confinement in the basket made the

pup's voice sound anywhere they'd a mind to fancy it.

"But how can it be a pup when they're all four here?" says March. "'Tis, though! Hear it!"

The pup grew more noisy. Hile, now shaking from his cap to his shoes, not with a smothered laugh this time, but with fear that he and his trick would be detected, saw there was only half a chance for him, and that was to let the yelper go. So he lifted the lid of the basket, and tumbled him out in the direction of the door, which was open, and close by, hoping he would run out, and give the boys a chase, so that he and Philete would have a chance to sneak away.

But the pup bumped his nose against the door-post, and then turned and ran back into the barn. So when the Goldins first saw him, it really looked as if he had just run in from the outside.

"I told you he was outside," says Sim Colby. And then there was more wonderment.

"It's the one we sold to Hile Hardack; must

be!" says Tobe. "But how did he find his way back here?"

"He never done it in this world!" says March.

"Dogs have wonderful instinct," says Sim.

"I know it," says March. "But this one's too young to travel that fur; an' his instinct ain't developed. I'd sooner think Hile fetched him here an' let him loose for the sake o' gittin' a day or two more keep out of us."

Then followed such an inventory of the Hardack mean traits, and such a raking down of the boys' characters, Hile's particularly, as would have made any decent chap squirm.

There was more wondering about both the dead pup and the live one; and when March said he'd give a silver dollar to know what caused the death of one, and how the other got back from Hardack's, Philete was tempted to come out, and give Hile away, and claim the reward. He certainly would have done it, if he hadn't been afraid of his brother.

"You see, if he ain't over here 'bout to-morrer night, inquirin' for his pup," says March.

"Then I s'pose he'll be a week longer luggin' him home agin."

Then the Goldins and their friend started to go, but when they got to the door they stopped to talk again. Hile, a little time before, had reached out his hand, preparatory to making a leap and cutting for home, in case they happened to look under the sleigh. His arm was still in the straw, when March, stepping back to let Sim Colby go out first, set his foot and his whole weight — cowhide boots, nails in the heel — right on to three fingers of Hile's hand. You could have heard 'em crunch!

There was one who did hear and feel them, too. That was the owner of the fingers. He would rather not have owned them just then. How he kept from yelling out I don't know. But he didn't make a sound, and there March stood and talked, and finally made a pivot of his heel, giving a grinding twist to those poor fingers, as he turned to see that the lantern had set nothing afire in the barn. Hile thought he never *would* get off, and believed he *must* yell; but he held in. I told you, to begin with, there was pluck in these Hardacks, though 'twas generally shown in a mean cause. Or possibly Hile had less feeling in his flesh and bones than most people have, just as he was kind of numb and dead in his moral nature.

He had feeling enough, though, with the biggest of the Goldin boys making mince-meat of three fingers of his right hand. When March finally stepped off, Hile was hardly aware of it, for any relief he got; he could pull his hand away, but the awful ache came away with it. When you have a tooth out the agony's over in about three seconds. But let a doctor tug away at your jaw a minute or so, and then have the pain keep right on raging — "to be continued," like the stories in the papers, — and I guess you'll have a fair idea of Hile's case.

After the Goldins had gone, Hile and Philete did a heavy business growling about the broken eggs and the mashed fingers, — Philete sucked what was left of the eggs, and Hile sucked what remained of his fingers, — and they crawled out from under the sleigh.

"I'd a plaguy sight druther all them eggs had

been inside o' me than out," says Philete. "My shirt an' waiz'ban's is jes' buttered with 'em!"

"Who cares for the eggs?" snarled Jehile. "Guess you wouldn't think about them, if you'd had a big, stout lummox standin' an hour 'n' a half on your hand, as I had!"

"Will you lug home one o' the pups?" says Philete.

"Blast the pups!" says Hile. ("Wish I had a rag," says he.) "They've seen 'em all back, an' they'll miss one if I take him now, an' know where he's gone to," says he. Then he went to sucking his bruised fingers again.

"You've got to gi' me that jackknife jest the same," says Philete. "An' thirty but'nuts to make up for the eggs I've got daubed with."

"Go to grass with yer jackknife an' but'nuts an' eggs!" says Hile in a fury.

Well, he didn't carry home a pup that night; he wouldn't have felt much like it, with such fingers, even if he had dared to do it. Besides, he had another idea.

Next day March overhauled Philete on the road,— very likely Philete was waiting round to be overhauled, — and asked him about Hile's pup. Philete looked down at his clothes, — all yellow and stiff-starched with the eggs he had wallowed in, — and acted as if he could tell something if he chose to do so.

"Come, Philete," says March, "out with it, an' I'll pay ye!" For he knew just how to manage a Hardack.

"Will ye gi' me that dollar?" says Philete.

"What dollar?" says March. Then he remembered, and the whole thing seemed to come to him. "Philete," says he, "was you or Hile in our barn las' night?"

"Gi' me the dollar," says Philete, grinning and looking foolish, "and promise not to let on to Jehile 't I told ye."

March didn't give him a dollar, but he did give him something, and promised; then Philete made a clean breast of it, — that is, as clean as a breast so stuck up with his share in the business could be.

March went home and told his brothers, and they had a hearty laugh over the joke of the Hardacks' being in the barn and Hile's getting his fingers squashed; though they were mad enough at Hile for being so careless with the pup. They went out and found the ruined hens'-nests and the crushed egg-shells, and had hardly got done laughing, — they'd just wiped the tears out of their eyes and got the kinks out of their sides, and were wondering what Hile would do about the pup now, — when they saw him coming to the barn with his empty basket in one hand and the other done up in a sling.

"Hallo, Hile!" says March, cheerful as could be. "What's the matter 'th yer hand?"

"Tell ye bime-by," says Hile. "Ye seen anything o' that 'ere pup?"

"What pup?" says Tobe.

"The pup I bought," says Hile. "He got away las' night an' run off, an' I've looked everywheres for him. Didn't know but he'd found his way back here," said he, telling that iron-clad lie with no more appearance of shame or guilt in his face than there was in the lid of his basket.

"Your pup's come home," says March; "but he's dead."

"Sho!" says Hile, opening his eyes. "I don't see how that can be!"

"Nor I," says Tobe, " 'thout somebody's legs 'sides his own fetched him. Or mabby the journey was too much for him. Sorry for ye, Hile."

"Oh, now, come!" says Hile. "It can't be my pup that's dead; le' me see!" He faced out the thing so, and was so positive one of the other pups was his, that the boys, out of sheer good-nature, let him have it.

"Be careful ye don't smother it in that basket," says Tobe, ready to split with giggling. "Don't ye think a meal-bag 'ud be safer?"

"Smother him! what ye mean?" says Hile, still innocent. "Oh, I sha'n't smother him!" says he.

"But ye hain't told us about your hand," says March, trying to keep sober, and about half succeeding.

"Oh, that!" says Hile. "The pup bit it when he got away from me las' night."

"I'm astonished!" says March. "He's only jest got his puppy-teeth. I shouldn't s'pose they could make any more dents *than the nails in the heel of my boot!*"

At that the boys shouted. All but Hile. He stared, as if wondering what the fun could be about, and then said, with a face as hard as that of a stone cherub such as they used to carve on monuments, —

" Wál, 'twan't much of a bite, but I put some sa've on 't, an' done it up, fear o' hyderfoby."

He went off with his pup, to get what good out of him he could, — if good can ever be got out of a thing come by in that way ; while the Goldin boys just keeled over and kicked and rolled on the barn-floor. He knew well enough what that meant.

PAUL GARWIN'S CHRISTMAS EVE

CHRISTMAS came on Sunday that year. Saturday evening was accordingly Christmas Eve; and there was one good man, at least, to whom that circumstance gave a double satisfaction.

Mr. George Garwin had come home from his noisy place of business, to his tranquil fireside, enjoyed his well-served six-o'clock dinner, and settled down comfortably to his newspaper, thankful that it was the end of the week and that another Christmas Eve found him alive and prosperous, with all his family about him.

He heard the door-bell ring faintly, but did not mind it until a servant came to say there was a man at the door who wished to speak with him.

"What name?" said Mr. George Garwin.

"He didn't give his name. He said he wished to see you just a minute on business."

"On business!" said Mr. George Garwin, and the face so bland and satisfied before became darkened by a frown.

For in Mr. George Garwin there were two really quite distinct men: the man of business, and the man of home and society. The first, exact and exacting, upright, prompt and often stern; the second, about as genial a friend and indulgent a father as any you will meet between one Christmas and another.

Mr. George Garwin liked to keep these two individuals entirely separate, and was always annoyed when he found his twin selves getting a little mixed.

"On business!" he repeated, laying down his paper, dropping the glasses from his nose, and going to the entry with a harsh, forbidding countenance, not at all calculated to cheer the humble person he found there.

That person was a grimy mechanic, who stood hat in hand, his head of short, bristling, black hair bowed in a rather abashed manner under the brilliant gaslight, his wet boots planted on the elegant soft carpet, and clusters of newly fallen snowflakes melting on his soiled and sombre clothing.

"Warson!" Mr. George Garwin exclaimed, staring at the intruder. "What are you *here* for?"

"If you please, sir," began the man, — "I beg your pardon, sir, — I am sorry to be obliged to ask it."

The look and voice of Mr. George Garwin embarrassed him so that his voice here became lost in an incoherent stammer.

"To ask what?" demanded Mr. George Garwin.

"Money, sir!" said the poor man.

"Money!" echoed Mr. George Garwin. "How happens it that you come *here* for money?"

"It's only my dues I am after," said the man Warson, plucking up courage, speaking more firmly. "My week's wages, if you please, sir."

"I don't understand this," said Mr. George Garwin, with his hands behind him, his chin out in a very arrogant attitude. "My cashier has orders to pay every man every Saturday night every cent due him. I draw checks for him. That's all I have to do with any man's wages."

"That's true, sir," said Warson. "And sorry I am to trouble you; but I was off this afternoon for two hours, on account of my child's sickness, and when I got back to the shop, the cashier said I was too late; he had locked up his safe. He said it was your orders to lock that always at half-past six."

"He was right!" said Mr. George Garwin. "It's the rule: we must have rules, and we mustn't allow them to be broken. I have another rule: never to transact business out of business hours. I can do nothing for you till Monday. Then you shall have your wages."

"It's a sorry word you speak for me and my poor family. And to-morrow Christmas of all days!" said Warson with a tremor in his voice. "But if you say it, I don't expect it will be unsaid. I know you for a hard man, Mr. Garwin!"

PAUL GARWIN'S CHRISTMAS EVE. — Page 168.

"If you know me for a hard man, don't come to me on such errands," said Mr. George Garwin with a singular change in his look and voice. "But I never expected a workman of mine would say that!"

Warson went away, reluctant and dissatisfied; and Mr. George Garwin — his business-self sadly mixed up with his domestic-self, to the manifest detriment of both walked back to his sitting-room and evening paper.

Then Mrs. George Garwin, who had overheard the talk in the entry, and had a glimpse of the snow-flaked, grimy mechanic, said in a tone of quiet pathos, —

"The poor man really looked as if he needed the money. I am sorry you couldn't give it to him."

Mr. George Garwin was feeling a good deal disturbed by Warson's last words, and he was glad of an opportunity to defend himself.

"So am I sorry! But it won't do to break over my rule. If I *begin* to let my men come after me here on business matters, there'll be no end to it. Shop is one thing, home is another. And I mean to keep the two distinct."

"Of course, you are right," said Mrs. George Garwin; "but it did seem as if this was an exceptional case."

"I can't make exceptions. I must treat all alike. This will teach him to toe to the mark in future. I'll teach him, too, not to be impudent!"

Mrs. Garwin wanted to say something about the man's sick child, but forebore, seeing how much her husband was annoyed. And having, by his last remark, quieted his conscience, — if it was that which had been disturbed, — Mr. George Garwin resumed the reading of his evening paper.

In about half an hour Mr. George Garwin, his domestic-self now well disentangled from the other, looked up cheerfully, and asked about the children's presents. Being told what purchases had been made for them, and that the girls were even then in another room plotting surprises for their parents and their brother Paul, he smiled approvingly, and asked, —

"Where's Paul?"

"Paul hadn't spent the five dollars you gave him for Christmas; and he went out a little while ago, I think, to buy something."

"Let's see what he will do with his money," said Mr. George Garwin, with a pleasant laugh. "Paul is shrewd! Paul is nobody's fool! We'll see!"

At the end of another half-hour, having examined some of the presents, particularly those which had been bought in his name, and talked in a genial, glowing manner about the great comforts of life with which they were blessed (*they* had no sick child), he again inquired, —

"Where's Paul? Hasn't he come in yet?"

"That must be his step now!" said Mrs. Garwin, quietly putting out of sight a skating-cap she was embroidering.

The hall door opened; somebody was heard shaking snow from an overcoat in the entry; then a ruddy-faced boy of fifteen came and looked into the sitting-room.

"Come in, Paul!" cried Mr. George Garwin. "Let's look at you! I want to know if you have found a use for your money?"

Paul entered hesitatingly, with an embarrassed smile.

"What did you buy?" said his mother.

For answer he gave an apologetic shrug, and threw up his empty hands.

"What! nothing?" cried his father.

"I suppose you'll think I've been very foolish," said Paul, looking rather ashamed as he took a seat with his damp boots at the register. "But I believe you said I could do just what I pleased with that five dollars."

"Certainly; taking it for granted that a boy of mine," said Mr. Garwin, "would do nothing silly or extravagant."

"Oh, I haven't been extravagant; and I hope you won't think I was very silly. And I'm going to tell you just what I've done with that money, if I can think how to begin."

Mr. Garwin looked at his son anxiously, but with an indulgent expression which encouraged him to go on.

"The truth is, as I was going along the street, two men were walking just before me, and I heard one of them ask the other to lend him a little money. To-morrow being Sunday — and Christmas, too — he must borrow a little, he said, or he couldn't have the heart to go home to his wife and children."

"I hope you haven't been giving money to a tramp on the street!" exclaimed Mr. George Garwin. "How often have I told you that every tramp is a liar, a thief in disguise!"

"I thought of that," said Paul, stammering a little. "But I didn't believe this man was a tramp. He couldn't have made up such a story — it was so straightforward" — the boy's eyes glistened — "and so touching! He was a laboring man of some sort. He had been disappointed in not receiving some money due him; and his children had been sick; and if he couldn't borrow, or get credit somewhere, his family must actually go hungry on Christmas, of all days in the year."

Mr. George Garwin knitted his brows, not with disapproval of what his son was telling him, but with a stinging recollection of his own conduct towards the man Warson an hour before.

"He, too, spoke of a sick child," thought he. "I might have given him something if it hadn't been for my business rules, and if he hadn't been insolent. Go on, my son."

"I hope I didn't act *too* impulsively," said Paul, crossing his feet on the register. "But when he said that, I couldn't help thinking how much *we* have of everything that is good, and how little my five dollars would be missed here at home!"

"Well, well, my boy!"

Mr. George Garwin coughed to clear his throat, while the mother regarded Paul with eyes full of pride and affection.

"I didn't know just what to do," said Paul, going on with more confidence. "His friend couldn't lend him anything, and he turned down the next street saying he would try to get credit at a store where he had traded sometimes, though he didn't seem to have much hope that he would succeed. Then I stepped forward, and said to his friend, —

"Do you know that man?"

"Yes," he said; "I know him very well,

and an honest fellow he is; and it's a shame that he should be in such a condition of a Saturday night, and Christmas Eve!"

"How happens it," I said, "that an industrious, sober man can't get a living, so as to be a little more independent?"

"My boy," he said, "*you* don't know anything about the lives of laboring men. He gets twelve dollars a week; but what is twelve dollars a week for supporting a family of six children with one or two of them sick half the time, and the wife worn out with work and watching? How *can* he get anything ahead?"

"Of course I couldn't answer that. So I just asked the man's name, and where he lived. I thought I would see for myself *how* he lived, if I could.

"Well," said Paul, after a moment's pause, "I found the place without much trouble, and, O father, *such* a place for an honest family to live in! All crowded together in one or two rooms; the mother, sick herself, with a sick child in her arms; one or two of the others crying — I couldn't help thinking, what if we were obliged to live in that way."

"I'm glad — I'm glad" — Mr. Garwin cleared his throat again — "that you took the precaution to see for yourself. But what — what excuse did you make for calling there?"

"Oh, I had a very good excuse. I knew Mr. Thomas wasn't at home, so I asked for Mr. Thomas. I said I couldn't wait to see him, and hurried away."

"Didn't you give the poor woman any money?" Mr. Garwin anxiously inquired.

"I couldn't somehow have a face to do that, though I thought afterwards I might have left the money for her husband; wouldn't he have been puzzled, but a good deal more glad than puzzled, when he got home?

"I thought of another plan. I went to the nearest grocery and bought some tea and coffee and sugar and crackers and a couple of loaves of bread; then to the next provision store, where I bought a fat turkey, and all the white potatoes and sweet potatoes and apples I could get for the rest of my money. I ordered all these things sent to the house; and I guess Mr. Thomas, if he has got home, is astonished by this time!" Paul added with a radiant smile.

"O my son!" exclaimed Mrs. Garwin with a gush of love and gratitude.

Mr. Garwin gave a slow, emphatic nod of approval. "You did right to satisfy yourself with regard to the family's circumstances before giving them help," he said. "And really, my boy, I don't see but that you managed very well — indeed, admirably! Did you send any name with the provisions?"

"Yes; I thought Mr. Thomas ought to know who sent them."

"You gave your name? That was right."

"No," said Paul; "I sent them in *your* name, father."

"In *my* name, Paul!" said Mr. Garwin, surprised. "But that wasn't right! That wasn't true."

"Let me tell you, father," said Paul, with something like an imploring look on his fine young face. "You gave me the money. I know you said I was to do what I pleased with it; but I couldn't have done *that* without it.

And, really, father, I *had* to say, 'A Merry Christmas, from Mr. George Garwin.' I'll tell you why: this man is one of your own workmen."

"What!" said Mr. Garwin with a start.

"Yes; and he was making a bitter complaint against you when I overheard him."

"What did he say?"

"I don't like to repeat it," said Paul. "Don't lay it up against him, will you? He was disappointed and desperate."

"Tell me what he said!"

"He said — he said — you passed for a decent sort of man, but you had no mercy on a poor laborer, with your iron rules. Rather than break one of them, you would let his children starve."

Mr. George Garwin compressed his lips and betrayed no little agitation as he replied, —

"I have no such man as Mr. Thomas at work for me. This must have been Warson."

"It was Warson, Mr. Thomas Warson," Paul admitted. "I was afraid to mention his full name at first. But now I will tell you everything. I was in the house when he called here this evening, and, forgive me, father, when I saw him and heard him speak, I felt sure that you were unjust — unjust to yourself, I mean; for we know that you are not hard or unfeeling.

"So I followed him out, and heard him talk with his friend on the street; and, father, I couldn't bear to have anybody speak as he did of you; so I thought the things *ought* to go in your name; and I hope you will think so too."

"You are right; you are right, my boy, every time!" Mr. George Garwin exclaimed with emotion. "I *was* too short with the man. We ought always to give a poor man's claims generous consideration. I thank you, my dear boy!"

"Oh, yes, Paul; and I thank you!" said his mother. "You have made me so happy!"

As for Paul, he could say nothing for the tears of joy and affection which choked his voice. He had never known so happy a Christmas Eve.

Sophie May's Complete Works

ANY VOLUME SOLD SEPARATELY

"GROWN-UP" BOOKS

DRONES' HONEY: A Novel $1.50

"GIRLHOOD" BOOKS

THE QUINNEBASSET SERIES
6 VOLUMES ILLUSTRATED PER VOLUME, $1.50

The Doctor's Daughter	Our Helen
Quinnebasset Girls	The Asbury Twins
In Old Quinnebasset	Janet; a Poor Heiress

LITTLE FOLKS' BOOKS

LITTLE PRUDY STORIES
SIX VOLUMES ILLUSTRATED PER VOLUME 75 CENTS

Little Prudy	Little Prudy's Cousin Grace
Little Prudy's Sister Susie	Little Prudy's Story Book
Little Prudy's Captain Horace	Little Prudy's Dotty Dimple

DOTTY DIMPLE SERIES
SIX VOLUMES ILLUSTRATED PER VOLUME 75 CENTS

Dotty Dimple at her Grandmother's	Dotty Dimple at Home
Dotty Dimple Out West	Dotty Dimple at Play
Dotty Dimple at School	Dotty Dimple's Flyaway

LITTLE PRUDY FLYAWAY SERIES
SIX VOLUMES ILLUSTRATED PER VOLUME 75 CENTS

Little Folks Astray	Aunt Madge's Story	Little Grandfather
Prudy Keeping House	Little Grandmother	Miss Thistledown

FLAXIE FRIZZLE STORIES
SIX VOLUMES ILLUSTRATED PER VOLUME 75 CENTS

Flaxie Frizz'e	Little Pitchers	Flaxie's Kittyleen
Doctor Papa	Twin Cousins	Flaxie Growing Up

An Illustrated Catalogue of "Sophie May's Stories" sent by mail postpaid on application

LEE AND SHEPARD PUBLISHERS BOSTON

LEE AND DOLLAR
L. SHEPARD'S D. JUVENILES

Comprising the following New Books and New Editions in attractive
English cloth binding and illustrated Any volume sold
separately $1.00 per volume

THE CASTAWAY STORIES 6 vols
Adrift in the Ice Fields   The Arctic Crusoe
Cast Away in the Cold   The Prairie Crusoe
Willis the Pilot   The Young Crusoe

FAMOUS BOY SERIES 4 vols. Illustrated
The Patriot Boy A popular life of George Washington
The Bobbin Boy The Early Life of Gen. N. P. Banks
The Border Boy A popular life of Daniel Boone
The Printer Boy or How Ben Franklin made his Mark

FRONTIER CAMP SERIES 4 vols. Illustrated
The Cabin on the Prairie By Dr. C. H. PEARSON
Planting the Wilderness By JAMES D MCCABE Jun.
The Young Pioneers By Dr. C. H. PEARSON
Twelve Nights in the Hunter's Camp By Rev. Dr. WILLIAM BARROWS

GALLANT DEEDS LIBRARY 4 vols. Illustrated
Great Men and Gallant Deeds By J. G. EDGAR
Yarns of an Old Mariner By MARY COWDEN CLARKE
Schoolboy Days By W. H. G. KINGSTON
Sand Hills of Jutland By HANS CHRISTIAN ANDERSEN

INVINCIBLE LIBRARY 4 vols. Illustrated
The Young Invincibles By I. H ANDERSON
Battles at Home By MARY G. DARLING
In the World By MARY G. DARLING
Golden Hair By Sir LASCELLES WRAXHALL Bart.

LIFE-BOAT SERIES of Adventures 5 vols. Illustrated
Dick Onslow among the Red Skins By W. H. G. KINGSTON
The Young Middy By F. C. ARMSTRONG
The Cruise of the Frolic A Sea Story By W H. G. KINGSTON
The Life Boat By R M. BALLANTYNE
Antony Waymouth By W. H. G. KINGSTON

Sold by all booksellers and sent by mail postpaid on receipt of price

LEE AND SHEPARD Publishers Boston

LEE AND SHEPARD'S DOLLAR JUVENILES

Comprising the following New Books and New Editions in attractive English cloth binding and illustrated Any volume sold separately $1.00 per volume

DARING-DEEDS SERIES 6 vols. Illustrated
Daring Deeds of the Old Heroes of the Revolution
The Old Bell of Independence and Other Stories of the Revolution
The Father of his Country A Young-Folk's Life of Washington
The Friend of Washington A Young-Folks' Life of Lafayette
The Great Peace-Maker A Young-Folks' Life of Penn
Poor Richard's Story A Young-Folks' Life of Franklin

THE LIVE BOYS' SERIES 6 vols Illustrated
Live Boys in Texas
Live Boys in the Black Hills
Paul and Persis
Young Trail Hunters
Crossing the Quicksands
Young Silver Seekers

NATURAL HISTORY SERIES By Mrs. R. LEE Illustrated by HARRISON WEIR 5 vols.
Anecdotes of Animals
Anecdotes of Birds Reptiles and Fishes
The African Crusoes
The Australian Crusoes
The Australian Wanderers

THE WILD SCENES LIBRARY 5 vols. Illustrated
Wild Scenes of a Hunter's Life
Noble Deeds of American Women
Pioneer Mothers of the West
Gulliver's Travels
Æsop's Fables

OLD ROUGH AND READY SERIES 6 vols. Illustrated
Old Rough and Ready Young Folks' Life of General Zachary Taylor
Old Hickory Young Folks' Life of General Andrew Jackson
The Little Corporal Young Folks' Life of Napoleon Bonaparte
The Swamp Fox Young Folks' Life of General Francis Marion
The Mill-Boy of the Slashes Young Folks' Life of Henry Clay
The Great Expounder Young Folks Life of Daniel Webster

GOOD AND GREAT SERIES 6 vols Illustrated
Good and Great Men
Women of Worth
A Quaker among the Indians
The Whales We Caught
House on Wheels.
Inn of the Guardian Angel

AROUND THE WORLD LIBRARY By Jules Verne
Round the World in Eighty Days Wreck of the Chancellor
A Winter in the Ice

DORA DARLING LIBRARY
Dora Darling
The Year's Best Days
Dora Darling and Little Sunshine

Sold by all booksellers and sent by mail postpaid on receipt of price

LEE AND SHEPARD Publishers Boston

LEE AND SHEPARD'S SEVENTY-FIVE CENT JUVENILES

Comprising new editions of the following popular Juveniles Bound in best English cloth bright colors Any volume sold separately

CHARLEY AND EVA STORIES By Miss L. C. THURSTON
How Charley Roberts became a Man
How Eva Roberts gained her Education
Home in the West
Children of Amity Court

> Miss Thurston writes with a purpose. She is an admirer of manly boys and womanly girls, and so carries her characters through scenes and situations that elevate and purify. The books are by no means slow, being full of adventures.

GOLDEN PROVERB SERIES By Mrs. M. E. BRADLEY
and Miss KATE J. NEELY
Birds of a Feather
Fine Feathers do not make Fine Birds
Handsome is that Handsome Does
A Wrong Confessed is Half Redressed
One Good Turn deserves Another
Actions Speak Louder than Words

> Two capital story-tellers, "birds of a feather," have flocked together, and produced from six old proverbs six as bright and taking story-books as ever gladdened the hearts of Young America; showing, indeed, that "handsome is that handsome does."

GOLDEN RULE STORIES By Mrs S. C. B. SAMUELS
The Golden Rule   Nettie's Trial
The Shipwrecked Girl   The Burning Prairie
Under the Sea   The Smuggler's Cave

CELESTA'S LIBRARY for Boys and Girls
Celesta   A Thousand a Year
Crooked and Straight   Abel Grey
The Crook Straightened   May Coverley

> Mrs. Samuels has written many attractive books. The scenes and incidents she portrays are full of life, action, and interest, and decidedly wholesome and instructive.

SALT-WATER DICK STORIES By MAY MANNERING
Climbing the Rope   The Little Spaniard
Billy Grimes's Favorite   Salt-Water Dick
Cruise of the Dashaway   Little Maid of Oxbow

> Not all tales of the sea, as the title of the series would imply, but stories of many lands by a lady who has been a great traveller, and tells what she has seen, in a captivating way.

UPSIDE-DOWN STORIES By ROSA ABBOTT
Jack of all Trades   Upside Down
Alexis the Runaway   The Young Detective
Tommy Hickup   The Pinks and Blues

VACATION STORIES for Boys and Girls 6 vols.
Illustrated
Worth not Wealth   Karl Keigler or The Fortunes
Country Life   of a Foundling
The Charm   Walter Seyton
        Holidays at Chestnut Hill

GREAT ROSY DIAMOND STORIES for Girls
6 vols. Illustrated
The Great Rosy Diamond   Minnie or The Little Woman
Daisy or The Fairy Spectacles The Angel Children
Violet a Fairy Story   Little Blossom's Reward

…'d by all booksellers and sent by mail postpaid on receipt of price

LEE AND SHEPARD Publishers Boston

HISTORICAL BOOKS
FOR YOUNG PEOPLE

Young Folks' History of the United States
By THOMAS WENTWORTH HIGGINSON. Illustrated. $1.50.
The story of our country in the most reliable and interesting form. As a story-book it easily leads all other American history stories in interest, while as a text-book for the study of history it is universally admitted to be the best.

Young Folks' Book of American Explorers
By THOMAS WENTWORTH HIGGINSON. Uniform with the "Young Folks' History of the United States." One volume, fully illustrated. Price $1.50.

"It is not a history told in the third person, nor an historical novel for young folks, where the author supposes the chief characters to have thought and said such and such things under such and such circumstances; but it is the genuine description given by the persons who experienced the things they described in letters written home." — *Montpelier Journal.*

The Nation in a Nutshell
By GEORGE MAKEPEACE TOWLE, author of "Heroes of History," "Young Folks' History of England," "Young Folks' History of Ireland," etc. Price 50 cents.

"To tell the story of a nation like ours in a nutshell, requires a peculiar faculty for selecting, condensing, and philosophizing. The brevity with which he relates the principal events in American history, does not detract from the charming interest of the narrative style." — *Public Opinion.*

Young People's History of England
By GEORGE MAKEPEACE TOWLE. Cloth, illustrated. $1.50.

"The whole narrative is made interesting and attractive — in every way what a book of this kind should be in its clearness of statement, freshness of style, and its telling of the right ways." — *Critic.*

Handbook of English History
Based on "Lectures on English History," by the late M. J. GUEST, and brought down to the year 1880. With a Supplementary Chapter on the English Literature of the 19th Century. By F. H. UNDERWOOD, LL.D. With Maps, Chronological Table, etc. $1.50.

"It approaches nearer perfection than anything in the line we have seen. It is succinct, accurate, and delightful." — *Hartford Evening Post.*

Young People's History of Ireland
By GEORGE MAKEPEACE TOWLE, author of "Young People's History of England," "Young Folks' Heroes of History," etc. With an introduction by JOHN BOYLE O'REILLY. Cloth, illustrated. $1.50.

"The history is like a novel, increasing in interest to the very end, and terminating at the most interesting period of the whole; and the reader lays down the book a moment in enthusiastic admiration for a people who have endured so much, and yet have retained so many admirable characteristics." — *N.Y. World.*

Sold by all booksellers, and sent by mail, postpaid, on receipt of price

LEE AND SHEPARD Publishers Boston

YOUNG FOLKS' TROPHIES OF TRAVEL.

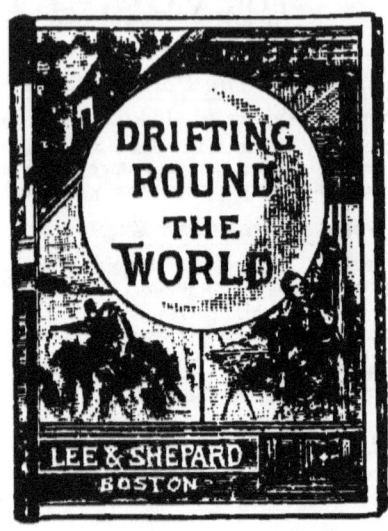

DRIFTING ROUND THE WORLD.
A Boy's Adventures by Sea and Land.
By CAPT. CHARLES W. HALL,

Author of the "Great Bonanza," "Adrift in the Ice Fields," etc.

200 illustrations. 384 pages. Royal 4to. Illuminated sides, $1.75. Cloth, full gilt, $2.50.

This tells the story of a boy's adventures by sea and land with a spice of newness and interest that will commend it to the young and make it a favorite everywhere. It has some two hundred illustrations, and not a page that a boy would skip as he listens to the skipper tell his wonderful story. It is a spleudid gift book.

OUR BOYS IN INDIA.

The Wanderings of Two Young Americans in Hindostan, with their exciting adventures, on the Sacred Rivers and Wild Mountains.

By HARRY W. FRENCH,

Author of "OUR BOYS IN CHINA."

With 145 illustrations. Royal octavo, 7 x 9½ inches. Bound in emblematical covers of Oriental design, $1.75. Cloth, black and gold, $2.50.

The great Indian Empire is the champion land for romance and adventure. In this story a little Yankee lad is kidnapped from his home. By the aid of a detective, an older brother, a lad of sixteen years, traces him to India. The adventures of the two, one as a captive and the other as a rescuer, in different parts of the empire, are thrilling, dealing as they do with the natives, the snake charmers and jugglers, royal personages and mountaineers, tiger hunts, elephant and rhinoceros fights. The descriptions of scenery, customs and wonders are graphic and instructive. Many of the illustrations are from special photographs taken for the author while in India.

OUR BOYS IN CHINA.

The thrilling story of Two Young Americans, Scott and Paul Clayton, wrecked in the China Sea on their return from India, with their strange adventures in China. By HARRY W. FRENCH, author of "Our Boys in India." 150 illustrations. Royal 4to. Illuminated covers, $1.75. Cloth, back and gold. $2.50.

"Our Boys in China" depicts the adventures of two young Americans wrecked in the China Sea on their return from India, with their romantic wanderings through the Chinese Empire. After successfully starting the young heroes of his previous book, "Our Boys in India," on their homeward trip, the popular and remarkable story-teller has them wrecked in the China Sea, saved and transported across China, giving him an opportunity to spread for young folks an appetizing feast of good things in the land of Confucius. — *Quincy Whig.*

YOUNG AMERICANS IN JAPAN.
Or, The Adventures of the Jewett Family and their Friend Otto Nambo.

By EDWARD GREÉY.

With one hundred and seventy full-page and letter-press illustrations. Royal octavo, 7 x 9½ inches. Handsomely illuminated cover, $1.75. Cloth, black and gold, $2.50. A new edition of which is now ready.

Mr. Edward Greéy was a member of the famous expedition which in 1854 caused "the Land of the Rising Sun" to be opened to Eastern civilization. He afterwards returned to Japan, "living among its estimable people, studied their language and literature, and what they term, 'learned their hearts.'" He is thus qualified to be a trustworthy guide to this the youngest and oldest of nations. His pen-pictures of Japanese scenery and customs are graphic, and by the introduction of spicy conversation are made dramatic. Markets and bazaars, shaké shops and Buddhist temples, jiu-riki-shas and jugglers are all brought before the eye.

YOUNG AMERICANS IN THE WONDERFUL CITY OF TOKYO.

Further Adventures of the Jewett Family and their Friend Otto Nambo.

By EDWARD GREÉY,

Author of "Young Americans in Japan," "The Golden Lotus," etc. With one hundred and sixty-nine illustrations. Royal octavo, 7 x 9¼ inches, with cover in gold and colors, designed by the author, $1.75. Cloth, black and gold, $2.50. Royal octavo, 7 x 9¼ inches.

In the great city of the great Empire of Japan, which the Japanese themselves call wonderful, the Young Americans find new cause for wonder at the strange customs and curious sights. Under the guidance of "Oto Nambo," their stanch friend, they assist at a fire, dine at Tokyo restaurants, are entertained by amateur performers, visit all the points of interest, and meet with many adventures; but the most interesting part of the book to American boys will be the visits to and descriptions of the different trades, many of which are illustrated, and all of which are described, from the "seller of folding fans" to the maker of "broiled bean curd."

YOUNG AMERICANS AMONG THE BEAR WORSHIPPERS

Of Japan, Yezo and the Island of Karafuto. By EDWARD GREEY. Price, boards, $1.75; Cloth, $2.50.

Yezo formerly belonged to Japan, but was ceded to Russia in 1875. The people bear the same relationship to the Japanese as the Indians do to America. They are as "hairy as bears, never feel the cold, and live to be very aged." The various members of the Jewett family and their friend, Oto Nambo, contrive to see and tell a great deal of the manners, customs, sports, traditions, and religion of this unknown and singular people. The book is 7 x 9½ inches; handsome cover; contains 180 illustrations by native Japanese artists, and 304 pages. — *Herald of Truth.*

J. T. TROWBRIDGE'S NEW BOOK.

THE TIDE MILL STORIES.

Illustrated. Each volume, 16mo, $1.25.

PHIL AND HIS FRIENDS.
THE TINKHAM BROTHERS' TIDE MILL.
THE SATIN-WOOD BOX.
THE LITTLE MASTER.
HIS ONE FAULT.
PETER BUDSTONE.

www.ingramcontent.com/pod-product-compliance
Lightning Source LLC
Chambersburg PA
CBHW020915230426
43666CB00008B/1465